T0113892

BECOMING A WOMAN OF WONDER

OWNING YOUR IDENTITY AS A WARRIOR WOMAN IN CHRIST.

REBEKAH FARTHING

WestBow
PRESS®
A DIVISION OF THOMAS NELSON
& ZONDERVAN

WestBow Press books may be ordered through booksellers or by contacting:

WestBow Press
A Division of Thomas Nelson & Zondervan
1663 Liberty Drive
Bloomington, IN 47403
www.westbowpress.com
844-714-3454

Scripture quotations marked KJV are taken from the King James Version.

Scripture quotations marked WEB are taken from the World English Bible.

Scripture quotations marked ASV are taken from the American Standard Version.

Scripture quotations marked AMPC are taken from the Amplified® Bible, Copyright © 1954, 1958, 1962, 1964, 1965, 1987 by The Lockman Foundation. Used by permission.

ISBN: 978-1-6642-7991-9 (sc)
ISBN: 978-1-6642-7992-6 (e)

Library of Congress Control Number: 2022918434

Print information available on the last page.

WestBow Press rev. date: 10/17/2022

CONTENTS

ACKNOWLEDGEMENTS

Special thanks to all the Godly women throughout my life who have poured into me spiritually. Thank you to my parents, who set a firm foundation on biblical principles, as well as my husband, Jordan, who encourages me in my walk with the Lord every day.

FOREWORD

Becoming a Woman of Wonder is a wonderful way for female believers of all ages to learn more about chasing after God's own heart.

Who doesn't dream of being a super hero at times to right the wrongs of our world or just be able to fly through beautiful skies? Rebekah explores the weapons and tools we are given to fulfill our mission through the power of the Holy Spirit. She takes us on her own journey in martial arts as she showcases the Armor of God.

For mothers and daughters, *Becoming a Woman of Wonder* can be an invaluable tool to grow together, while each growing in their relationship with Jesus Christ.

-Diane Darocha, a servant in youth and children's ministry for over 30 years.

INTRODUCTION

Hello! Are you ready to become a woman of wonder? I encourage you to take your time with this study. Let all the information sink in. Don't just rush through to see how fast you can complete it. I speak as one who likes to get things done yesterday, but trust me, you'll get more out of it if you take your time. Since you've decided to pick up this book, I'm guessing you desire a deeper relationship with the Lord. Hopefully, this will help you to live in the reality of who God says you are, guide you in the use of all the gifts and weapons He has given you, and present you with new ideas on how you can walk out your mission on earth: to be more like Jesus every day. The activities included in each chapter are intended to provoke thought, so I hope that you accomplish them with the intent of learning, rather than just checking off a box. Feel free, also, to make notes of what God is speaking to you personally as you go through this study. He speaks to us all differently, so you might get something out of it that no one else did; a word just for you!

Before we begin this journey, it's imperative that you come with a clear line to the Father. He is is our ultimate teacher and the one that will guide you and speak to you. This study is just a tool that I pray He chooses to use. Change always comes when we make a step toward God in surrender and ask Him to shape us. It starts by laying aside every weight that would hold us down — the ones that hinder our prayers and keep us from seeing victory in our life. Psalm 66:18 KJV says, "If I regard iniquity in my heart, the Lord will not hear me." The iniquity David speaks of can be any bitterness, unforgiveness, unconfessed sin, anger, pride, or jealousy we hold on to that keeps us from that victory. All of what we are about to discover and do is moot if we do not have a clear connection to the Father. Take a moment to go before God, asking Him to search your heart and make you clean — to reveal to you anything you need to confess.

Here is your time. Use this space to write a prayer to the Father:

We are human. We will sin, often without even knowing. The searching of your heart and confession should be a daily part of your prayer. Coming before Him every day to humble yourself is what it means to walk humbly with God.

Let's pray together.

Dear Father,

I thank you for the words of this study. I thank you for the truths that you are revealing to your people. I am grateful that you have created us to be warrior women. I ask that you open our heart to hear and understand what you want us to learn. Lord, bless these dear women that are looking to you for their strength and their joy. I thank you that you are always at work in us and for us, fighting our battles. I pray we would learn to co-labor with you to be the female warrior princesses you've destined us to be. In Jesus's name we pray, Amen.

If I were able to be with you all, I'd have hot coffee and teas set out for you with a plethora of flavored creamers. Chex mix would be on the tables with a bowl of M&M's and some apple slices, and soft praise music in the background would prepare our spirits while we approach the Father. I have compiled my Women of Wonder playlist for you all to be strengthened and encouraged throughout this journey.

"The Same Power" By Jeremy Camp
"You Say" By Lauren Daigle
"Every Giant Will Fall" By Rend Collective
"Warrior" By Hannah Kerr
"Fearless" By Jasmine Muray
"Resurrection Power" By Chris Tomlin
"The Comeback" By Danny Gokey
"More Then Conquerors" by Rend Collective
"Unfinished" By Mandisa
"Love Them Like Jesus" By Casting Crowns
"Overcomer" By Mandisa
"Born For This" By Mandisa
"What You're Worth" By Mandisa
"Warrior" By Steven Curtis Chapman
"Crazy Faith" By John Waller

Enjoy!

CHAPTER 1
IDENTITY

DISCOVERY

Who are you? Do you know?

Every kingdom has a king. There is a royal blood line. There are important titles given to people. There is rank. The kingdom of heaven is much like this. There is one King and ruler over all — God the Father. There is a royal bloodline — Jesus's blood, which runs through the veins of all those who believe. There is rank — the Bible tells us we are ranked above the angels, who even have ranking system within the angelic realm.

Here on Earth, whenever a person of royalty is to be introduced, it's customary to say their title, name, lineage, and where they're from. It would look something like this: Princess (title) Jasmine Smith (name), daughter of King Christopher (lineage) of Bethelania (country of origin). We have a title, a name, a lineage, and a country of origin as well. But do we know it? Do we live in the realization of it?

> So God created man in his *own* image, in the image of God created
> he him; male and female created he them.
> (Genesis 1:27 KJV)

> But ye are a chosen generation, a royal priesthood, an holy nation,
> a peculiar people; that ye should shew forth the praises of him who
> hath called you out of darkness into his marvellous light.
> (1 Peter 2:9 KJV)

> And will be a Father unto you, and ye shall be my sons and
> daughters, saith the Lord Almighty.
> (2 Corinthians 6:18 KJV)

By the truth of these verses, we will begin to write our story.

Who does God say you are? Look at 2 Corinthians above. You are His daughter, which means you belong to His kingdom. In 1 Peter, we see you have been chosen. You were lovingly placed in this day and age — a time that the prophets of old only dreamed about. What a blessing!

You are royalty. By being adopted into the kingdom of God you have all the rights of a child of God because you are one!

> And if children, then heirs; heirs of God, and joint-heirs with Christ; if so be that we suffer with him, that we may be also glorified together.
>
> (Romans 8:17 KJV)

You were made in the likeness of God (Genesis 1:27). You weren't made in the likeness of a monkey or an angel or anything else on the Earth or above the Earth or under the Earth. You were fashioned in the image of God.

If I were to ask you who you are, what would you say?

"I am_____."

Fill in the Blanks

Genesis 1:27 (KJV): "So God created _____ in His own image; in the image of _____He created him; male and female He created them".

1 Peter 2:9 (KJV): "But _____are a _____ generation, a _____ priesthood, a _____ nation, His own _____ people, that you may proclaim the praises of Him who called _____ out of darkness into His marvelous light".

2 Corinthians 6:18 (KJV): "I will be a Father to _____, and _____ shall be My sons and _____, Says the Lord Almighty".

Answer this question by writing your name, preceded by your title. Yes, you have a title. In case you don't know, it's princess.

Who are you?

_____

FROM WHENCE WE CAME

For you formed my inmost being. You knit me together in my mother's womb.

(Psalm 139:13 WEB)

The Spirit of God has made me; the breath of the Almighty gives me life.

(Job 33:4 WEB)

The Spirit of God — God Himself — made you. He formed you in your mother's womb, breathing life into you. You are not a weed that came up by chance because the wind blew the seed there. You are a flower — purposely planted in a particular soil during a particular season for a particular reason. You were created for a divine purpose by the divine creator.

He isn't served by men's hands, as though he needed anything, seeing he himself gives to all life and breath, and all things.

(Acts 17:25 WEB)

You have granted me life and loving kindness. Your visitation has preserved my spirit.

(Job 10:12 WEB)

He is the very one who gives us life. Not only does He give us the first breath we take, but He also enables us to keep breathing. It's easy to go about our daily lives taking every day for granted when really, every day is a gift — so we should live like it is.

One way is to constantly give praise for all the things He has given you throughout the day, no matter how big or small. The new international version for Job 10:12 uses the word "providence" instead of visitation, which means, "God as the guide and protector of all human beings." Even though you can't see Him, He is constantly there. He is protecting you from the things you cannot see.

> All things were made through him. Without him, nothing was made that has been made. In him was life, and the life was the light of men.
>
> (John 1:3-4 WEB)

So why did He form you? He did not create you so He could be served by human hands. We were created for fellowship with the Creator. Not as slaves, but as sons and daughters.

> No longer do I call you servants, for the servant doesn't know what his lord does. But I have called you friends, for everything that I heard from my Father, I have made known to you.
>
> (John 15:15 WEB)

Fill in the blanks.

Psalm 139:13 (WEB) "For you formed _____ inmost _____. You knit _____ together in my mother's womb."

Job 33:4 (WEB) "The Spirit of God has made _____; the breath of the Almighty gives _____."

Acts 17:25 (WEB) " He isn't served by men's hands, as though he needed anything, seeing he _____ gives to _____ and _____, and _____ things."

John 1:3-4 (WEB) "_____ were made through him. Without _____, _____ was made that has been made. In him was life, and the_____ was the light of men."

Job 10:12 (WEB) "You have granted me _____ and _____. Your visitation has preserved my spirit."

Where did you come from?

_____

YOU ARE NOT A WEED
THAT CAME UP BY
CHANCE. YOU ARE A
FLOWER PLANTED
ON PURPOSE.

DON'T HIDE YOUR IDENTITY

In the popular DC Comics series *Wonder Woman*, the heroin appears in the United States for the first time after living on a secluded island all her life. She came in full Amazonian garb. She looked odd, as you can imagine. She got a lot of weird stares and people kept their distance. Just picture a five-foot-ten woman walking downtown with a short leather battle skirt, knee-high boots, a breast plate, shield, and a sword.

She was peculiar. The word peculiar means "strange" or "odd". But it also means "belonging exclusively to, having the characteristics of, representative of, [or] unique to." This is what Diana (Wonder Woman) was to Themyscira (the place she is from). She had the characteristics of the people of Themyscira, such as their height, their hair, and their style. She was a representative of her kingdom and her people.

> But ye are a chosen generation, a royal priesthood, an holy nation,
> a peculiar people; that ye should shew forth the praises of him who
> hath called you out of darkness into his marvelous light;
> (1 Peter 2:9 KJV)

We are peculiar to God and His kingdom which means we should have the characteristics of kingdom people. We are the representatives of the kingdom of heaven to the people of earth. We were made in His image for the purpose of showing His praise to others. We know who to thank for our lives, our being, and every good thing. We should show it.

> The glory which you have given me, I have given to them; that
> they may be one, even as we are one; I in them, and you in me,
> that they may be perfected into one; that the world may know
> that you sent me and loved them, even as you loved me. Father, I
> desire that they also whom you have given me be with me where I
> am, that they may see my glory, which you have given me, for you
> loved me before the foundation of the world.
> (John 17:22-24 WEB)

We were given His glory. The Greek word for glory is *Doxa*. It refers to the nature and acts of God in self-manifestation; what He is and does, as well as the manifested perfection of character and righteousness, of which all people fall short. What this means is He has given us the ability to perform the acts He did and walk in the newness of Christ with His nature rather than our sin nature.

> Most certainly I tell you, he who believes in me, the works that I do, he will do also; and he will do greater works than these, because I am going to my Father.
>
> (John 14:12 WEB)

He has clothed us with robes of righteousness.

> But now apart from the law, a righteousness of God has been revealed, being testified by the law and the prophets; even the righteousness of God through faith in Jesus Christ to all and on all those who believe. For there is no distinction, for all have sinned, and fall short of the glory of God; being justified freely by his grace through the redemption that is in Christ Jesus;
>
> (Romans 3:21-24 WEB)

> I will greatly rejoice in the LORD, my soul shall be joyful in my God; for he hath clothed me with the garments of salvation, he hath covered me with the robe of righteousness, as a bridegroom decketh himself with ornaments, and as a bride adorneth herself with her jewels.
>
> (Isaiah 61:10 KJV)

He did all this so that we could be in fellowship and unity with Him. He did it so the world would know that God, out of His great love for us, sent Jesus. We look like Him so that the world can see Him. How else will they know unless they are shown?

> For, "Whoever will call on the name of the Lord will be saved." How then will they call on him in whom they have not believed? How will they believe in him whom they have not heard? How will they hear without a preacher? And how will they preach unless they are sent? As it is written: "How beautiful are the feet of those who preach the Good News of peace, who bring glad tidings of good things!
>
> (Romans 10:13-15 WEB)

You came from heaven to bring good news!

Complete the verses below.

"But ye are a _____generation, a _____ priesthood, an _____ nation, a _____ people; that ye should shew forth the praises of him who hath called _____ out of darkness into his marvellous light;" (1 Peter 2:9 KJV)

"The glory which you have given me, I have given to them; that they may be _____, even as we are one; I in them, and you in me, that they may be _____ into one; that the world may _____that you sent me and _____ them, even as you loved me. Father, I desire that they also whom you have given me be with me where I am, that they may see my glory, which you have given me, for you loved me before the foundation of the world." (John 17:22-24 WEB)

"For, "Whoever will call on the name of the Lord _____ be _____."" How then will they call on him in whom they have not believed? How will they believe in him whom they have not heard? How will they hear without a _____? And how will they preach unless they are _____? As it is written: "How beautiful are the feet of those who preach the Good News of peace, who bring glad tidings of good things!" (Romans 3:21-24 WEB)

Answer these questions.

What does peculiar mean?

_____

Besides Heaven what or who are you a representative of?

_____

How does this effect the choices you make?

_____

How should being a representative of Heaven effect your choices?

_____

In your own words describe what it means to you to have Jesus give you His glory.

_____

_____

_____

_____

_____

Write a prayer thanking God for your adoption and His providence. Let Him know what it means to you to be His child.

_____

_____

_____

_____

_____

WARDROBE

Going back to our Wonder Woman analogy, the way Wonder Woman dresses when she came to the States immediately gives her away. She's not a native to say the least. Her escort brings her to a dress shop where she tries on many garments. While trying on her first dress she questions, "How can a woman possibly fight in this?" And on the third one, "It's itchy, it's choking me".

Should this not be our verbiage as well? As princesses of the King, we are not of this world. When we wear the world's clothes they should be very uncomfortable. The clothes of the world are: lust, greed, pride, deceit, fleshly desires, and all the actions that stem from them. Our reactions to these should be like Diana's responses towards the dresses, "How can a woman possibly fight in this?" When we are wearing the world's clothes, we cannot effectively fight spiritual battles. By wearing the clothes of the world, we literally handicap ourselves. We cannot hear the still small voice of the Lord and He won't hear us. Yikes!

> If I regard iniquity in my heart, the Lord will not hear.
> (Psalm 66:18 ASV)

To regard iniquity in your heart is to have a sin and keep it and be unwilling to deal with it. You have placed it in your heart and refuse to let it go.

> But your iniquities have separated between you and your God, and
> your sins have hid his face from you, that he will not hear.
> (Isaiah 59:2 ASV)

What a scary thought! To be separated from God, our lifeline, our source of strength, our guide.

I had just moved to Ft. Myers, Florida and was driving around downtown at ten o'clock at night. A big parade had just finished and everyone was packing up and leaving. Being newer to the area, I wasn't so familiar with all the roads yet … and by that I mean that I only knew one way to get home … which just so happened to be blocked by the parade route. To top it off, there was absolutely no signage for how to take a detour.

I thought, "Ok. You can figure this out."

After turning on a few one-way roads, I was lost. I turned on my phone to try to get my GPS working. No signal. Just my luck. I had explored all my immediate solutions to no avail. So, I did what any 18 year old does when caught in a bind, I called my mom. She was 800 miles away. I wasn't sure what else to do. She began trying to locate where I was by using a map and whatever indications I could give her as to how I got to where I was. She was not being calm to say the least. My brother got on the line and tried to instruct me, in a less than pleasant tone, on the proper way to use my phone and get my GPS working. It didn't help. Meanwhile, my father, who is an Inspector of Aircraft, was in the background looking up the flight pattern in case he had to borrow a plane and come get me. (Yeah, that's my dad for you.)

In the meantime, mom had gotten my grandpa on another line to try and help. He used to be a navigator in the Navy, so she thought he could navigate me out. I don't think cars work on land the same way ships work on water. When mom, dad, and brother started to argue, I hung up the phone and continued driving.

Of course, there were no street signs. After driving around, trying to find the biggest roads with the most light, I finally found a highway and managed to get a hold of a Florida friend that ensured me I was on the right path. I apparently had taken a turn and ended up in the worst part of town. There, I had lost my connectivity. The fear of not knowing where I was and having silence from my GPS was not fun to say the least.

This is what we do when we wear the clothes of the world (lust, greed, pride, deceit, fleshly desires, etc.). These are the wrong turns that will lead us into the bad parts of town where there is no signal; where you lose your spiritual connectivity.

Dear sisters, I pray if you find yourself going down the wrong roads that you will cry out and repent. Repent means to stop and turn the opposite direction — that you will not regard iniquity in your heart so that you may be spiritually re-connected to a place where there is a voice and direction from the Father.

What should we wear? What are the clothes befitting for a Princess of the king? Thankfully the Bible lays these out for us.

> Likewise, you younger ones, be subject to the elder. Yes, all of you clothe yourselves with humility, to subject yourselves to one another; for "God resists the proud, but gives grace to the humble.
>
> (1 Peter 5:5 WEB)

When we talk to people what is our motive? We're normally talking to show how much we know about the topic or trying to make ourselves appear smart. This is pride, the opposite of humility.

> Now deck yourself with excellency and dignity. Array yourself with honor and majesty.
>
> (Job 40:10 WEB)

Dignity is being worthy of honor or respect.

What are the clothes of the world?

_____

_____

_____

_____

The Lord will not hear me if I do what actions?

_____

_____

What separates us from God?

_____

What are the clothes of Heaven?

_____

What does it look like to clothe yourself with Dignity?

_____

What is dignity?

_____

Are my actions worthy of honor and respect?

_____

What are some of the actions that stem from wearing the clothes of the world?

_____

_____

_____

What will our actions look like when we are dressed in Heaven's garments?

_____

_____

_____

UNDER ARMOR

> But put on the Lord Jesus Christ, and make no provision for the
> flesh, for its lusts.
>
> (Romans 13:14 WEB)

This verse can be kind of confusing if, like I did, you thought, "How do I put on a person?" when it says, "put on the Lord Jesus Christ". Ever talk to someone and say, "Ooh! That's a nice dress." And they respond with something like, "Thank you. It's Calvin Klein". The Lord Jesus Christ is the designer. He designed every good and perfect thing. So, to wear Him is to wear the clothes He designed and in so doing, outfit ourselves for battle.

What are these garments? They are righteousness, love, peace, and thankfulness to name a few.

> I will greatly rejoice in Yahweh! My soul will be joyful in my
> God, for he has clothed me with the garments of salvation. He
> has covered me with the robe of righteousness …
>
> (Isaiah 61:10 WEB)

> Above all these things, walk in love, which is the bond of perfection.
> (Colossians 3:14. WEB)

Love brings all the virtues together. If we want to represent Jesus, we need to look like Him, look like heaven. Wear His clothes.

What's the one thing you put on that you don't dare leave the house without?

I'm sure phone, keys and wallet/purse are on that list, but my number one would be … Underwear! Or, if we're being prim and proper, we would call them "foundational garments". If we have love as our foundation, as the one thing we don't dare forget when we go about our day, it will change how we view everything.

But now faith, hope, and love remain—these three. The greatest
of these is love.

(1 Corinthians 13:13 WEB)

What are some ways you can show love to others today? We all show love in different ways and feel love in many ways.

… Out of the abundance of the heart the mouth speaks.

(Matthew 12:34 WEB)

As a first step, we should speak with love. When responding to people, do so graciously even if what they are saying is off the wall or annoying. I'm working on this and it's not easy. Sometimes you want to shake people, but we need to understand that they were not given the same knowledge we have or the same experience. We have been given the light of Jesus. The truth has been made known to us. Everyone who has not experienced salvation is living in the dark. Being rude, impatient and unloving to non-believers for their missteps is like scoffing at a blind person for missing their mouth when they eat. The love we must have is a super natural love and can only come from above. Ask God to give you His love for other people. His love is lasting and pure. If we don't have God's love, we don't have any love to give.

"Above all these things, walk in _____, which is the bond of
_____.". Colossians 3:14

"But now _____, _____, and _____ remain—these three.
The greatest of these is _____" 1 Corinthians 13:13 WEB

What are the garments of heaven?
_____

FRAGRANCE

Another thing I really hope NO ONE forgets is deodorant. Deodorant makes you smell good. It does so by blocking the sweat producing pores and masking our scent with something good. How you smell is also a reflection on your lifestyle and what you eat. If you eat a lot of onions or garlic or high fat foods, your body is going to sweat that out as a way of detoxing. This is all how we were designed to stay healthy but can be very unpleasant to the people around us. Your scent is one of the first things people notice about you. If you smell good, they notice. If you smell bad, then they really notice.

How you smell will determine if people want to be around you. Let the love of Christ be your fragrance. The love of Christ should be on the inside of you so what comes out of you is the fragrance of Christ. If we live on spiritual junk food it will come out when we're around people. Things you listen to, watch, read, and play will all effect how you speak and act.

> For we are a sweet aroma of Christ to God, in those who are saved
> and in those who perish.
>
> (2 Corinthians 2:15 WEB)

To God, we are the carriers of the aroma of Christ. Picture a room full of smelly things. We have the ability to be the Plug-ins that contain the refreshing, odor eliminating scent of Jesus, which we spread wherever we go.

I have a friend that has this certain scent of perfume and wears it quite heavily sometimes. I can tell if she's walked through the room or if someone has been in her presence. Shouldn't that be how our life is? That people would know by the way we "smell" that we've been in His presence. Should we not have the aroma of Christ?

2 Corinthians 2:15 (WEB) " For we are a _____
of Christ to God, in those who are saved and in those who perish:"

GAINING GROUND

He said to them, "Go into all the world, and preach the Good
News to the whole creation.

(Mark 16:15 WEB)

You didn't choose me, but I chose you and appointed you, that you
should go and bear fruit, and that your fruit should remain; that
whatever you will ask of the Father in my name, he may give it to you.

(John 15:16 WEB)

Go and make disciples of all nations, baptizing them in the name
of the Father and of the Son and of the Holy Spirit, teaching them
to observe all things that I commanded you. Behold, I am with
you always, even to the end of the age." Amen.

(Mathew 28:19-20 WEB)

There's something to be said about hiding and staying safe. There is also something to be said
about pushing forward. In scripture we are given the command to *go and do*. The world doesn't
need another person who is going to hide in a fox hole. They need a warrior — someone who will
inspire others and be an example to light the way. Someone who looks different, sounds different,
and walks different. You can be that person. You can be the shift in your school, your workplace,
or your family. Wherever you go, you are an ambassador. You are a Light Bearer. You are to bring
the good scent of Jesus to a stinky world. You are a victor because you have clothed yourself in
Christ, who is our salvation.

But when this perishable body will have become imperishable, and
this mortal will have put on immortality, then what is written will
happen: "Death is swallowed up in victory.

(1 Corinthians 15:54 WEB)

In other words, when we, who are perishable, have been clothed with Jesus, the Imperishable, the saying becomes true. Death has been swallowed up in victory. We are no longer doomed to death and separation from Him, but receive eternal life and the promise of a new body on a new earth free of suffering, pain, and evil. He gives us the victory through our Lord Jesus Christ.

It's like playing a sport. If I want to have someone on the team, I give them a jersey. I clothe them with the team shirt, give them a welcome, and put their name on the roster. They now have all the privileges of a team member. The victory plays out like the game Othello. In this game, white or black pieces will surround the other color to turn them into their respective color. When all the black pieces surround a white piece it turns black and vice versa. Our goal is to take all the people of the world, introduce them to Christ, and let Him do the transformative work of their becoming a new creation; part of the kingdom of God.

> Come now, and let's reason together," says Yahweh: "Though your sins are as scarlet, they shall be as white as snow. Though they are red like crimson, they shall be as wool.
>
> (Isaiah 1:18 WEB)

The command to go and preach seems very daunting but we are not alone. He who has called us is faithful to keep His promises. Remember the way God uses you to spread the gospel is unique to the way He made you to be. Not everyone is given the gift of evangelism, or teaching, or prophesy. How you spread the gospel is going to be between you and God. Ask Him how you can be most effective in doing the work of the kingdom. There's no score chart in heaven over who won the most souls. It doesn't effect your salvation and it doesn't effect God's love for you. God requires your obedience. Just listen for what He tells you to do.

> I will instruct you and teach you in the way which you shall go. I will counsel you with my eye on you
>
> (Psalm 32:8 WEB)

> Haven't I commanded you? Be strong and courageous. Don't be afraid. Don't be dismayed, for Yahweh your God[a] is with you wherever you go.
>
> (Joshua 1:9 WEB)

Rebekah Farthing

Has God placed an area of ministry on your heart?

What do you have a passion for?

_____

Isaiah 1:18 (WEB) " Come now, and let's reason together," says Yahweh: "Though your _____ are as scarlet, they shall be as _____ as snow. Though they are _____ like crimson, they shall be as _____."

"I will _____ you and _____ you in the way which you shall _____. I will _____ you with my _____ on _____" Psalm 32:8 WEB

PURPOSE

Our mission as Christians, let me re-phrase that: as daughters of Adonai, is to be His witnesses — ambassadors of the Kingdom of Heaven — introducing our Father's kingdom to those who have never seen it. This is our public service. The greatest thing we can do for someone is introduce them to Jesus. In the end only one thing matters. It doesn't matter how many memories you made, places you've seen, or things you own — what matters is your personal relationship with Christ.

What is our purpose? To have relationship with the Father, to fight for the lost that they might come to know Him, to be a defender of the weak, to uphold righteousness, seek justice, love mercy, and walk humbly with God. Sounds like a lot right off the bat, but it is very possible. By the power of the Holy Spirit, you can do these things!

There was a time in my life when I knew what the Bible instructed me to do and how I should act, but despite my desire to do everything right, I still found myself reacting in the flesh to things. I got so upset because I wanted to be perfect right then! I felt like Paul — who did the things he didn't want to do and didn't want to do the things he did. (Romans 7:15-25)

I would come home after a not-so-nice interaction with someone and just cry. I was trying to do things right but my flesh would get the best of me. I had no forgiveness for myself but let all the condemnation sink in. I was trying everything to achieve righteousness on my own. I was trying to sanctify myself. It was in a moment of breakdown that I realized at the uttermost root of my anger towards myself was a deep-seated pride issue. You see, I wasn't trusting God to do a work in me. I wanted it to be faster. I wanted to be sanctified and complete right then. I didn't want to ever have flesh issues. Wouldn't that make me look like a perfect Christian? Ha!

Truth is although I went to God with it, I wasn't trusting His process. In a moment of seeking, God said, "Do you think you can transform yourself better than I can?" I asked for forgiveness.

Every time I felt convicted that I had done something flesh-controlled, I would say I was sorry to the person I acted badly towards — then to God. I'd asked Him to help me. I thanked Him for convicting me and not giving up on me. I believe there was a lesson in here about learning to apologize and admitting my faults. He probably could have transformed me instantly but I believe he wanted me to learn that lesson.

Romans 7:24-25 into chapter 8 goes on to say,

> "Who will deliver me out of the body of this death? I thank God through Jesus Christ our Lord! So then with the mind, I myself serve God's law, but with the flesh, sin's law."

Basically, I desire to do right but I am flesh and sometimes I make a mistake so who will deliver me out of this state? God will!!.

> There is therefore now no condemnation to those who are in Christ Jesus, who don't walk according to the flesh, but according to the Spirit.
>
> (Romans 8:1 WEB)

We do not need to feel that condemnation! As long as we are following after the Spirit with our whole heart, there is forgiveness and most likely conviction when we go astray. This verse doesn't mean that we will never have a fleshy moment; it merely says, we don't walk by the flesh. We don't habitually choose to sin; we don't live in it and we aren't governed by it. We live in the Spirit. Thus, if we do something of the flesh, the Spirit will convict us but not condemn us. Then we repent and move on. We don't stay in it like a pig wallowing in the mud.

The Word says God chastises those He loves. People who are undisciplined are referred to as illegitimate sons. When I would teach karate, if someone had potential I would correct them more because I knew there was hope of refinement. If someone earnestly didn't want to be there and never changed what they were doing after correction I wouldn't correct them as much. It wasn't worth my time because they were not going to listen anyway. Correction is a sign of growth. The correction of the Lord isn't to strike you down and make you feel defeated, but to refine you, make you more effective to reach the world around you, and give you favor with God and man. My best advice is to learn to love correction. If you are going to be a follower of Christ, you will always be in a constant process of sanctification. At my house we say we are in a constant state of calibration.

It's time to walk out our purpose. How do we do this? I'll give you some ideas, but let's see if you can come up with some of your own. Take some time and write down your ideas.

_____

_____

To have relationship with the Father we need to talk to Him daily. If you need to have a scheduled time to separate yourself from the world and draw closer to Him, then do that. Eventually start talking to Him all the time throughout the day.

How do you fight for the lost? Intercede in prayer for people that need salvation. Talk to them. I know this sounds pretty simple but most of the time we are in our own little worlds, and we stay in our circle of friends. Ministering to people begins with relationship. It doesn't have to be deep but establishing that you're friendly and receptive is a good start. You might want to look into doing an outreach with your church. The lost won't normally come to you — you have to meet them where they're at. Just like Jesus.

Defend the weak. When you hear someone talking negatively about themselves or someone else don't let the Devil plant those seeds. Speak the truth of God's word into their life. This also takes knowing people on a deeper level. Not everyone will share their inner mind struggles with you. Be connected. Be a friend to someone. Have a circle of likeminded people that are encouraging each other toward a relationship with God. Be intentional about checking in on people. It is vitally important that gossip never flow out of your mouth. Also, in the practical sense, if you can help someone, do it.

Uphold righteousness. When there's gossiping happening withdraw yourself or even better say, "Hey, maybe we shouldn't talk about [said person]." When there's deceitful actions happening, stop them. Be a person of integrity. Lev 19:15 tells us not to show preference to people of wealth over the poor or vice versa. To uphold righteousness is to uphold justice. The Strong's concordance has this to say about righteousness, "the verbs associated with righteousness indicate the practicality of this concept. One judges deals, sacrifices, and speaks righteously; and one learns, teaches, and pursues after righteousness."

This can be a lot, but don't worry, we have help!

In your own words write out your purpose.

My purpose is to

_____

_____

Write down what changes you can make to your daily life to start walking out your purpose.

_____

_____

_____

THE GOOD FIGHT

Fight the good fight of faith. Take hold of the eternal life to which you were called, and you confessed the good confession in the sight of many witnesses.

(1 Timothy 6:12 WEB)

Let us look at this verse with the before and after verses to get a clear picture of the context of this text.

For the love of money is a root of all kinds of evil. Some have been led astray from the faith in their greed, and have pierced themselves through with many sorrows. But you, man of God, flee these things, and follow after righteousness, godliness, faith, love, perseverance, and gentleness. Fight the good fight of faith. Take hold of the eternal life to which you were called, and you confessed the good confession in the sight of many witnesses.

(1 Timothy 6:10-12 WEB)

Being a disciple of Christ and a "Kingdom Child" isn't a position to be lazy in. You have a purpose, you have a mission. You're a warrior. Verbs convey action. We need to take action. These are the actions 1 Timothy 6:11 tells us to take — fight, hold tightly, and confess. Fight and when you can't fight, hold on. To "lay hold" of something is to grasp it tightly. Paul is instructing Timothy to not let go of eternal life. Don't turn from the ways of the Lord and follow a different master. Confess and proclaim that you are a Kingdom Child. Don't hide under a bush.

Right after this, Paul writes in verse 14, "that you keep the commandment without spot, blameless, until the appearing of our Lord Jesus Christ,"

Take steps to walk out your salvation. In 1 Timothy 6:11 we are told to pursue righteousness, godliness, faith, love, patience, and gentleness of heart. All of this goes into fighting the good fight. Fight is an action verb. It requires we do something and in certain circumstances to refrain from doing.

Be courageous, and let's be strong for our people, and for the cities
of our God; and may Yahweh do what seems good to him.

(2 Samuel 10:12 WEB)

"Be strong for our people". Fighting the good fight is not just about keeping your salvation and being untainted, it's also about fighting for those who can't fight for themselves. One reason we are here is for training (we'll discuss that later). Another reason, which is the main point, is for other people. It's a Biblical principle. The second greatest commandment is to love one another as you love yourself. Jesus exemplified living for others. He was truly a servant even though He was Lord of all. Ponder these verses on caring for others.

Pure religion and undefiled before our God and Father is this:
to visit the fatherless and widows in their affliction, and to keep
oneself unstained by the world.

(James 1:27 WEB)

Each of you not just looking to his own things, but each of you
also to the things of others.

(Philippians 2:4 WEB)

Bear one another's burdens, and so fulfill the law of Christ.

(Galatians 6:2 WEB)

In love of the brothers be tenderly affectionate to one another; in
honor preferring one another;

(Romans 12:10 WEB)

So then, as we have opportunity, let's do what is good toward all men,
and especially toward those who are of the household of the faith.

(Galatians 6:10 WEB)

But if anyone doesn't provide for his own, and especially his own
household, he has denied the faith, and is worse than an unbeliever.

(1 Timothy 5:8 WEB)

Whoever stops his ears at the cry of the poor, he will also cry out,
but shall not be heard.

(Proverbs 21:13 WEB)

What is the religion that the Father accepts?

_____

What 6 things are we told to pursue?

_____

2 Samuel 10:12 (WEB) "Be _____, and let's be _____ for our _____, and for the cities of our God; and may Yahweh do what seems good to him."

Now go back through 1 Timothy and write down all the verbs.

_____

HOLY SPIRIT POWER

But you will receive power when the Holy Spirit has come upon
you. You will be witnesses to me in Jerusalem, in all Judea and
Samaria, and to the uttermost parts of the earth.

(Acts 1:8 WEB)

If we were to look upon the task of witnessing to all Jerusalem, Judea, and Samaria, which is like saying all of your county, your state, and your country, we would say, "No way! How am I supposed to do that? I do not have the qualifications. I don't know how." According to Acts we will receive the power when the Holy Spirit comes upon us. Still, it will not be all laid out for us in a clear, concise, step by step manual. It will be in the day to day surrendering and following that we will begin to walk out our purpose. Then, one day we will look behind us and realize how far the Lord has brought us.

Upon first reading Acts 1:8, I had some questions. Did the Holy Spirit come upon me and I missed it? When does it come upon me?

Peter replied, "Peter said to them, "Repent, and be baptized, every
one of you, in the name of Jesus Christ for the forgiveness of sins,
and you will receive the gift of the Holy Spirit.

(Acts 2:38 WEB)

It really is just as simple as asking. Many people don't know to ask because they've never been taught about the Holy Spirit, who He is, and what His purpose is in your life. The Holy Spirit is literally the spirit of God that dwells in you. Jesus said He must go so He can send us another, who will be our comforter. The Holy Spirit is a game changer and is God's anointing on your life to complete the calling He has on it. The Holy Spirit is the equipping that makes walking out the faith possible.

> John answered, saying unto them all, I indeed baptize you with water; but one mightier than I cometh, the latchet of whose shoes I am not worthy to unloose: he shall baptize you with the Holy Ghost and with fire.
>
> (Luke 3:16 KJV)

This was a baptism of repentance from sins. But the Holy Spirit was not available to them yet. The first-time people received the Holy Spirit was in John 20:21-22

> Jesus therefore said to them again, "Peace be to you. As the Father has sent me, even so I send you." When he had said this, he breathed on them, and said to them, "Receive the Holy Spirit!
>
> (John 20:21-22 WEB)

There are varying opinions about one baptism or two separate ones. Here is what I have come to believe as true. For a long time only the baptism of repentance was preached resulting in salvation. Nothing was being preached about the Holy Spirit. Perhaps because of a lack of understanding about Him. Thus, two baptisms would result. In the New Testament, Paul went to the disciples and baptized with the Holy Spirit.

> Now a certain Jew named Apollos, an Alexandrian by race, an eloquent man, came to Ephesus. He was mighty in the scriptures. This man had been instructed in the way of the Lord; and being fervent in spirit, he spoke and taught accurately the things concerning Jesus, although he knew only the baptism of John.
>
> (Acts 18:24-25 WEB)

> While Apollos was at Corinth, Paul, having passed through the upper country, came to Ephesus and found certain disciples. He said to them, "Did you receive the Holy Spirit when you believed?" They said to him, "No, we haven't even heard that there is a Holy Spirit." He said, "Into what then were you baptized?" They said, "Into John's baptism." Paul said, "John indeed baptized with the baptism of repentance, saying to the people that they should believe in the one who would come after him, that is, in Jesus." When they heard this, they were baptized in the name of the Lord Jesus. When Paul had laid his hands on them, the Holy

Spirit came on them and they spoke with other languages and prophesied.

(Acts 19:1-6 WEB)

Here we see that the two baptisms were merely because of a lack of knowledge about the Holy Spirit. It is possible to be saved and filled at the same time. As long as you believe in the Trinity and recognize your need for the Holy Spirit to reside in you and guide your life. He won't leave you empty.

> I will also give you a new heart, and I will put a new spirit within you. I will take away the stony heart out of your flesh, and I will give you a heart of flesh. I will put my Spirit within you, and cause you to walk in my statutes. You will keep my ordinances and do them.
>
> (Ezekiel 36:26-27 WEB)

The Holy Spirit gives us the ability to follow His decrees and keep His law. God knew that walking out His ways and denying the flesh would not be easy, so He sent help! I'm reminded of children who insist on doing everything on their own and refusing help. I believe this is how we are a lot of times. How much easier would it be if we accept that we have weaknesses and don't know all things and take the help? It's like game shows, we can call a friend! And as many times as we need to!

> The Lord Yahweh's Spirit is on me, because Yahweh has anointed me to preach good news to the humble. He has sent me to bind up the broken hearted, to proclaim liberty to the captives and release to those who are bound, to proclaim the year of Yahweh's favor and the day of vengeance of our God, to comfort all who mourn.
>
> (Isaiah 61:1-2 WEB)

That is a lot of things that God has called us and anointed us to do! Are we walking out our full potential?

> Yahweh's Spirit will rest on him: the spirit of wisdom and understanding, the spirit of counsel and might, the spirit of knowledge and of the fear of Yahweh.
>
> (Isaiah 11:2 WEB)

Now, knowing this we have no excuses. We've been given this Spirit, so it's time to claim it and live like it.

Acts 1:8 (WEB) "But you will receive _____ when the _____ has come upon _____. You will be _____ to me in Jerusalem, in all Judea and Samaria, and to the uttermost parts of the earth."

Ezekiel 36:26-27 (WEB) "I will also give you a new _____, and I will put a new _____ within you. I will take away the stony heart out of your flesh, and I will give you a heart of flesh. I will put my _____ within you, and cause you to _____ in my statutes. You will keep my ordinances and do them."

Isaiah 61:1-2 (WEB) "The Lord Yahweh's _____ is on _____, because Yahweh has _____ me to preach good news to the humble. He has _____ me to bind up the broken hearted, to proclaim _____ to the captives and release to those who are bound, to proclaim the year of Yahweh's favor and the day of vengeance of our God, to _____ all who mourn."

According to Isaiah 11:2 what Spirit do we have?

_____

Acts 2:38 (WEB) "Peter said to them, "_____, and be _____, every one of you, in the name of Jesus Christ for the forgiveness of sins, and you will _____ the gift of the _____.""

HOLY SPIRIT POWER PART 2

We are given the ability to do great things. When the Lord tells us to do something, we can because He anointed us to do it. He equips us by His Spirit. Jesus had the Holy Spirit without measure and that is why He could do all the miraculous things He did. That same spirit resides in you. There is no limit to what He can do through you. We have been made one with Christ. Without Him we can do nothing. In addition, when the Lord wants to do something He will move through you to accomplish it. Yes, He has the capability to create things out of thin air, but most of the time He works through His sons and daughters here on earth. When God wants to bless or speak to someone, He'll call us to action. He'll give us a word for a person or prompt us through the tugging of our spirit to give something to someone. This helps the receiver but it also helps you the giver. The Lord loves a cheerful giver and blesses the obedient. When He calls you to do something, He is literally inviting you to position yourself for a blessing.

We do not command the Spirit.
We are commanded by the Spirit.

The Spirit is a part of God that dwells within you and moves through you; to lead you and guide you, to communicate the will of the Father. Often, we tend to think of the Holy Spirit like our own personal genie. We summon up a good prayer and watch Him do our bidding. We think we can control the power of the Spirit. The Holy Spirit is a person, a part of the triune God head. That means He is sovereign because God is sovereign. The hand of God is not guaranteed to move because we do something or say the certain words or sing the right music. There are promises given to us in scripture and when we align our requests with His word we can know we are praying in His will. It is His will that none should perish but all would come to repentance. Praying for salvation is always good. We are commanded to pray for the sick that they might be healed. Even if we don't see the results immediately, or ever, we must believe in the sovereignty of God. He knows things we don't because He is omnipresent and omnipotent. He is everywhere all the time within time itself. We might not get the answer we want, but if we pray in His will, we can be confident that what we receive is what is the best for us. As we walk closer with God, the Holy Spirit will guide our prayers. Walk in His will and His ways and you will start to see the promises of God in your life.

The Holy Spirit makes His presence known in my life in a variety of ways. The Holy Spirit confirms things. For instance, when someone gives you a word for your life, does His presence show up? Sometimes in a sermon or a conversation the presence of the Lord, the Holy Spirit, can be physically felt. As if to say, "hey, I agree with this." At times He shows up in worship as a reminder that He does inhabit the praises of His people. I've felt His presence stirring pudding, washing dishes, at church … wherever I was praising Him. It doesn't matter where you are physically, it matters what the posture of your heart is. The Holy Spirit also is the one who keeps me from saying and doing foolish things. I have stopped cold turkey in the middle of a sentence and said, "Sorry. I can't finish, never mind". Because I felt this heaviness in my chest warning me that what I was about to say was unprofitable. Although it gets on people's nerves and leaves them wondering, it's a lot better to be in tune with the Spirit and shut my mouth then to have to repent for gossiping or slandering. My mother in law always tells me, "I don't gossip because then I'd have to repent and that's no fun." She's right.

In your own words describe the Holy Spirit. How does His Spirit residing in you effect your daily life?

_____

_____

_____

_____

When did the Holy Spirit come upon you?

_____

I am the _____God will use to pour out his _____ on earth.

We do not _____The Spirit. We are _____ by the Spirit

If you have never received the gift of the Holy Spirit now is a great time!!! All you have to do is ask. Pray this prayer with me and get ready to receive.

Dear Heavenly Father, thank you for the gift of your Spirit. I ask that you would fill me with your Holy Spirit. Baptize me with the Holy Spirit and fire. I receive all that you have for me right now in Jesus name. Thank you for filling me. Amen.

EMERGE

For if you remain silent now, then relief and deliverance will come
to the Jews from another place, but you and your father's house
will perish. Who knows if you haven't come to the kingdom for
such a time as this?

(Esther 4:14 WEB)

God created Esther for a purpose, He had a plan for her life. He chose a specific time and place in history in which to place her for the saving of His people. He has just as much interest in your life as He did with Esther's. He chose this exact time and place in history to breathe you into existence.

Have you ever heard that saying "Don't rock the boat"? Or "Don't awaken the lion"? Well, the boat's already rocked. The lion's awake! (1 Peter 5:8) If the evil one can keep you from knowing whose you are and keep you from hearing the voice of God, He has won because you'll never fight back. You are no longer a threat. No more! You are a princess of the Most High God, fashioned with armor, equipped with weapons, blessed with the power of the Holy Spirit! You can't afford to sit back and hide. The world needs you! God didn't create you to just sit here. He created you for such a time as this.

You have been anointed! God will teach you what He wants you to do. Sometimes we don't even realize He's schooling us until we've learned the lesson. God will surround you with the things that will help you know and fulfill your destiny. Don't be so busy with your own plans that you miss out on His. He desires to know you and abide with you, know Him and abide in Him.

I am the vine. You are the branches. He who remains in me and I
in him bears much fruit, for apart from me you can do nothing.
(John 15:5 WEB)

We think we can do a few things or the little things … we can do NOTHING! We get frustrated a lot because we try to do things on our own and fail. Or we do things without prayer first and then ask God to fix our problems. He loves us and will help us out, but still so much could be done and so many mistakes could be avoided if we abided in Him constantly. Isn't it easier to learn a lesson when you can talk to the teacher about it and discover whether you're even doing the homework right? This will come by abiding in Him, having constant fellowship with Him.

How can I discern what He wants me to do specifically? Abide in Him.

The world needs you because the world needs Jesus. And you are how He is going to get to them.

> Be sober, be vigilant; because your adversary the devil, as a roaring lion, walketh about, seeking whom he may devour.
> (1 Peter 5:8 KJV)

> As for you, the anointing which you received from him remains in you, and you don't need for anyone to teach you. But as his anointing teaches you concerning all things, and is true, and is no lie, and even as it taught you, you will remain in him.
> (1 John 2:27 WEB)

> For I know the thoughts that I think toward you," says Yahweh, "thoughts of peace, and not of evil, to give you hope and a future.
> (Jeremiah 29:11 WEB)

Using 1 John 2:27 answer the questions below.

You received what? _____

Where does it abide? _____

Who teaches you? _____

What are you being taught about? _____

What is our part? _____

CHAPTER 2
THE SWORD

THE SWORD

And take the helmet of salvation, and the sword of the Spirit,
which is the word of God.

(Ephesians 6:17 WEB)

We can't talk about fighting without discussing weapons. I am a practitioner and teacher of karate-do, meaning "empty hand way". Our style is called Shito-Ryu and one of the things that makes us unique is our five different weapons. I love my weapons. Having tools makes any job easier — and that's what weapons are, tools; tools for defending yourself and your freedom. The traditional Okinawan weapons that I train with were once farm tools that the people developed into weaponry for lack of anything else. Like the prongs used for tossing rice bails became sai, the handles for the grain mills- tonfa, and the sickle to cut grass- kama. We, as women of faith, have the armor of God. Our weapon being the sword of the Spirit. As we have just learned, we fight from the power of the Holy Spirit and God's written word. It is the key to our victory.

So many times, I heard the term "Sword of the Spirit" and thought the Spirit was fighting for us. I had it all wrong — our sword is the Word of God.

... and the sword of the Spirit, which is the Word of God.

(Ephesians 6:17 WEB)

This sword is the Word. Hebrews 4:12 KJV says, "For the Word of God is quick and powerful, and sharper than any two-edged sword, piercing to the dividing asunder of soul and spirit, and of the joints and marrow, and is a discerner of the thoughts and intents of the heart."

Whoo! Now that's powerful!

How do we use the Word as a weapon? While listening to Lisa Bevere I finally got it. You pray the scriptures. You do as the Father does, and say what He says. Find passages that pertain to your situation and pray God's word over it. You have a voice, use it.

More than a voice, you have authority. You have authority because you are under authority — God's authority. Just like a police man doesn't have authority on his own but he is under the authority of the local government or state, giving him the ability to make people abide by the law and fine them if they don't.

> He called to himself his twelve disciples, and gave them authority over unclean spirits, to cast them out, and to heal every disease and every sickness.
>
> (Matthew 10:1 WEB)

> Jesus came to them and spoke to them, saying, "All authority has been given to me in heaven and on earth.
>
> (Matthew 28:18 WEB)

Here we see that whatever authority man had at the beginning of creation and forfeited to Satan, Christ has won back. He is now the Champion, Ruler of the universe. In Matthew, He gave His Disciples authority. Let's check out Luke 10:19.

> Behold, I give you authority (Greek "exousia") to tread on serpents and scorpions, and over all the power (Greek- "Dunamis") of the enemy. Nothing will in any way hurt you.
>
> (Luke 10:19 WEB) (*Parenthesis added*)

It's very important to recognize the two separate words for power here. The first word for power used is "exousia". It means, "authority", "the ability or strength with which one is endued", "the right to exercise power", "the power of one whose will and commands must be obeyed by others", and "one who is subject to authority or rule." So, we have Jesus, ruler of the universe, giving us authority, the right as members of His blood line, to exercise His power. The ability and strength to trample on the enemy — and that enemy has to obey! We've got to get this.

Notice the word used for the enemy's power is not the same. It is not authority. Take a look. The word for power there is "dunamis". Strong's concordance states that dunamis "almost always points to new and higher forces that have entered and are working in this lower world of ours". That's all it is — a higher force that has entered our plain of existence and is at work to steal, kill, and destroy. (John 10:10)

The power that the enemy has over your life is only the power you give him. You have the power, the delegated authority, to protect yourself from anything that's harming you. The protection status of your life is in your hands. The power lies in the blood of Jesus. When He arose from the dead, He bridged the gap and offered adoption into the family of Christ, making us co-heirs with Christ, and giving us the authority to use His name. When you step out and operate in the authority you're given, you are acting as if Jesus was standing there right in that moment doing the very thing you are doing.

Jesus has done everything He needed to do. He gave you the authority so you can cast out demons in His name and lay hands on the sick that they would be healed. We are ambassadors. When we operate in the authority that God gives us, it is as though God was speaking Himself.

Constantly remind yourself of the authority you've been given. Stop accepting what the devil throws at you. Fill yourself with the truth of God's word so that you will know a lie when it comes. The Holy spirit will also give you discernment. Always be on your guard. When the enemy wants to manifest in your life, rebuke him. Have scriptures in your quiver like arrows ready to defend — that you would be able to tell the enemy, "It is written". Wield your sword!

What are some examples of verses you can pray into situations? Think of a problem in your life that could use some scripture breathed into it. Look up verses that you could use to pray over the situation. Write down the problem and the scripture to answer it.

_____

_____

_____

_____

_____

_____

_____

The sword is _____

Luke 10:19 (WEB) "" Behold, I give you _____ to tread on serpents and scorpions, and over _____ the _____ of the enemy. _____ will in any way hurt you."

"We fight from the power of the Holy Spirit and God's written word."

LIVING BY THE SWORD

> But ye, beloved, building up yourselves on your most holy faith,
> praying in the Holy Spirit, keep yourselves in the love of God,
> looking for the mercy of our Lord Jesus Christ unto eternal
> life. And on some have mercy, who are in doubt; and some save,
> snatching them out of the fire; and on some have mercy with fear;
> hating even the garment spotted by the flesh.
>
> (Jude 20-23 ASV)

Jude 20-23 gives us 5 Key points to living a life of a warrior.

The 5 points are:

1. Build yourself up by praying in the Spirit.
2. Keep yourselves in God's love.
3. Have mercy to those who doubt.
4. Save others by snatching them from the fire.
5. Hate corruption.

Point 1: praying in the Spirit. There have been different interpretations of this, but I'm going to say be willing to be led by the Spirit in your prayer life. Be open to praying in tongues as the Spirit leads.

> These signs will accompany those who believe: in my name they
> will cast out demons; they will speak with new languages.
>
> (Mark 16:17 WEB)

Sometimes there are no known words you can express, but the Spirit will pray through you in a heavenly language. Other times the Spirit will tell you what to pray in your own language. Either way, be open to His leading.

Point 2: "Keep yourself in God's love". Well, what does that mean? Let's break it down. What is God's love? The word for love here is "agape". Strong's dictionary says "it expresses the deep and constant love and interest of a perfect being towards entirely unworthy objects." God's love is not fickle, it is not determined by our actions, God's love is there — always.

> For I am persuaded that neither death, nor life, nor angels, nor principalities, nor things present, nor things to come, nor powers, nor height, nor depth, nor any other created thing will be able to separate us from God's love which is in Christ Jesus our Lord.
>
> (Romans 8:38-39 WEB)

If His love isn't determined by our actions and nothing can separate us from that love, why do we have to keep ourselves in God's love? I spent a few days praying about this and discussing it with my Spirit-filled husband, and this is what was revealed to us. God's love is constant and always there, but we have a choice whether to stay in it and receive it. No person or thing can separate us from His love, but He does give us a choice to receive it. Think of rain or a water spout. It is there, it is available to stand under, but you can move out of it. Here is an example of a real life application. You are following the Lord; seeking to do right. All of a sudden, you find yourself amongst your friends and they are participating in activities you know are not right. You don't want to make them feel bad or appear holier-than-thou, so you don't say anything. Maybe you even join in to try and fit in, but the next day you feel horrible. The guilt you have weighs heavy and there's a small voice that says, "You are unworthy to go before the throne in prayer. Why are you worshipping? He knows what you did. You're a filthy sinner." You then remove yourself from an active relationship with the Lord. You walk out of and reject His love towards you because you know your actions weren't right and you feel condemned. This is right where the enemy wants you — out of touch with the Father. In the Father's love there is forgiveness and mercy.

To keep yourself in God's love is to stay moldable and humble. To admit when you are wrong and accept His forgiveness. God's love for you is greater than any mistake you can make.

> Even as the Father has loved me, I also have loved you. Remain in my love. If you keep my commandments, you will remain in my love; even as I have kept my Father's commandments, and remain in his love.
>
> (John 15:9-10 WEB)

Did you catch that? " … If you keep my commandments, you will remain in my love …" Jesus knew that if we followed His commandments, we would not feel the guilt and shame that would cause us to remove ourselves from His love.

Point 3: "Be merciful to those who doubt." A lot of times it is our flesh nature to look down on or judge those who don't see the way we do or believe what we believe especially if we were brought up in the church. People of other religions or no religion at all are not so different than we are. For example, women of the Muslim faith are told they must always cover their head, as is their belief, while In the Old Testament Jewish women were told to cover their heads. We're not that far from them. We must be careful not to cast judgement because the only reason we are able to believe in the Lord and see the truth is because the Holy Spirit has revealed Himself to us and gives us wisdom and understanding. He can, and has, done the same for them.

> No one can come to me unless the Father who sent me draws him,
> and I will raise him up in the last day.
> (John 6:44 WEB)

> When he (the Holy Spirit) has come, he will convict the world
> about sin, about righteousness, and about judgment.
> (John 16:8 WEB)

We only know what is true by the Spirit of the Lord.

> However when he, the Spirit of truth, has come, he will guide you
> into all truth, for he will not speak from himself; but whatever he
> hears, he will speak. He will declare to you things that are coming."
> (John 16:13 WEB)

We can see by these verses that we have no reason to boast or think more highly of ourselves then we ought for it is only by the grace of God that we have the knowledge of Him. We must therefore have mercy for those who have yet to receive the truth. We must continue to pray for them and show them the love of God, meanwhile, keeping our truths at heart. It is completely possible to be friendly to someone but not believe the same. I would caution to be aware of who you let in your inner circle and who you receive life advice from. Always surround yourself with people that are farther ahead on the Christian walk than you are so that they will build you up and not bring you down. Be the influencer to those around you and be choosy about who you let influence you. Paul even instructed Timothy to protect the truth given to him.

> Timothy, guard that which is committed to you, turning away from
> the empty chatter and oppositions of what is falsely called knowledge,
> which some profess, and thus have wandered from the faith.
> (1 Timothy 6:20-21 WEB)

Point 4: "Save others by snatching them from the fire". The "fire" here is a metaphor for hell. We know that all who deny the Lord will be separated from Him and not be given the gift of eternal life in the presence of the Lord. Here we are given the command to show others the Lord: to share the gospel and introduce them to Jesus.

Point 5: "Hating even the clothing stained by corrupted flesh". In all of our commands to love people we are told very clearly to hate corruption. This goes further to say even the clothing stained by corrupted flesh. Basically, the slightest bit of corruption we need to abstain from. There is no room for contamination. One rotten egg in a batch of a 100 scrambled eggs will make everyone sick. We want to be pure vessels for the Spirit to flow through. This means we will have to be careful of what we allow ourselves to do, hear, and see. Yes, the world needs to know what we are for, but in the midst of this we can't lose sight of what we are to stay away from. The world needs to see that we are following what we preach and living it out.

> Because it is written, "You shall be holy; for I am holy.
> (1 Peter 1:16 WEB)

We are to be imitators of Christ. We must be if we want to truly walk in the fullness of all God has for us; to not just be mediocre Christians, but world changers and mountain movers.

It's important to practice using your sword. Just like faith without works is dead, having a sword but keeping it in the closet is dead to you as well. Practicing spiritual swordsmanship daily is something we all have to work on. Don't be discouraged if you don't master it in a day. It takes time. I once started learning how to use the Samurai sword. I found that I would first have to be dressed in full karate garb. Then I needed to make sure my belt was tied in just the right place with the right amount of tightness. Now that I was dressed, I could begin. Just getting the sword out of the sheath and back without stabbing myself or dropping the scabbard proved to be a challenge, let alone doing it with speed and accuracy. Needless to say, that is an art I will not be performing anytime soon. In karate we must practice our katas (forms) daily so that when we are asked to perform them, we can do so with ease and the face of a warrior — and so it is with speaking the Word. If you don't practice speaking the Word or at least reading it daily to familiarize yourself with it, you will not be able to use it when needed. Norman Schwarzkopf once said, "If you sweat in the peace, you won't bleed in the war." And my wise Souke (Grand Master) always said, "Cry in the dojo (training hall) but laugh on the street". Read the Word daily, pray in the Spirit, practice your swordsmanship. We know we are going to face trials and temptations. We know we will come against evil and need our swords. What we don't know is the exact time. That is why it is important to be alert and ready. The enemy scours the earth looking for those he can devour. Eventually the predator will find prey. We are supposed to be protectors of God's people, of our families, of our church … Even if we aren't personally being attacked, we can't stand by and watch our brothers and sisters fall. We refuse to be prey — we are the ones who pray.

Write down the 5 points to living a life of a warrior.

1)_____

2)_____

3)_____

4)_____

5)_____

What stuck with you the most about today's lesson?

_____

_____

How changes can you make to start living out the 5 points?

_____

_____

We refuse to be prey — we are the ones who pray.

THE SECOND SWORD

Wielding the sword isn't just about praying "scary prayers" as Lisa Bevere calls them. Those would be the ones where you speak directly to the enemy and rebuke him — calling out the evil by name. There is another type of sword — the sword of praise and worship. Praise and worship is all throughout the word of God. Many times, in the Old Testament the worshippers were sent out ahead of the army and in one case, while they were praising the Lord, the Lord caused a confusion to fall upon the enemy and the enemy slaughtered one another. Another time they marched around singing praises and walls literally came down! Recall Paul and Silas who, while singing praises, were delivered from their jail cells. Worship can take us from this earthly thinking into focusing on God. It is exalting God's name above everything. As we declare His goodness and mercy the problems of this world fade away and all that is left is the beauty of His love.

What does praise do? The job of praise is to minister victory above impossible situations. That is the outcome of Biblical praise we should expect. That as we praise, God works out the victory in our situations. As we draw near to God, He draws near to us, and we embrace in the middle. When God meets us, He meets us with all that He is. He is healing. He is provision. He is a protector. He is our Deliverer. Expect the victory.

The greater the realization of who He is, the greater our worship will be. Praise changes your perception. It is the telescope we use to view God. What seems small when we are far away is so much bigger than we can imagine. Does praise make God bigger? No. God is the same size, His abilities are the same every day. It is our perception of Him and what He is doing, and can do — both in and through us — that changes.

Worship is the gateway to the throne room. It brings us face to face with our Creator. It brings us into the presence of the Prince of Peace, where we feel perfect peace. There is no worry, there is no strife. From this position we are renewed by a dose of His spirit and newness of life. Worship is our communing with God. Worship is where we can lay our hearts before Him and He responds. Yes, He has every right and ability to know what is in our hearts, but He desires for us to tell Him about it.

I know my husband loves me and thinks I'm beautiful, but I still want to hear Him tell me. Worship is a little more than human experiences can define but that is as close of a representation

I can get at the moment. Worship is spiritual intimacy. It's an action between two beings; you and God. Here are some of the benefits of worship laid out in scripture.

> And ye shall serve the LORD your God, and he shall bless thy bread,
> and thy water; and I will take sickness away from the midst of thee.
>
> (Exodus 23:25 KJV)

If ever we could use a blessing on our food and water, it's now.
Romans 12:1 instructs us to worship with our whole self,

> Therefore I urge you, brothers, by the mercies of God, to present
> your bodies a living sacrifice, holy, acceptable to God, which is
> your spiritual service.
>
> (Romans 12:1 WEB)

The amplified bible says "act of worship" instead of spiritual service. Worship isn't just something we do but who we are. Our lives are supposed to be worship. This means offering up everything we do in service to Him as our act of worship. Offering what we make with our hands and where we go with our feet. We are on a mission for Him. Even if it's to the grocery store. You never know who is there that might need a glimpse of Jesus. You are that glimpse. You are the salt of the earth.

PAUSE! *Side lesson here. As a Christian, how many times have you heard to be the salt? What does that even mean? Well, salt isn't just a flavoring; although it is the most important seasoning if you ask me. Jesus didn't say make this world more palatable. Salt is a preserver. It stops the decay or spoiling process. That's what Christians are supposed to be doing. Preserving the earth. Keeping the Dark One at bay. Our prayers and our worship stem the tide of this war we are in. We are in a spiritual battle. We've got to fight for our family, our friends and our fellow man.*

Okay, back to the main message.

By living a life of worship, you are living a life of surrender. Everything you do is not for your glory but God's.

> Whatever you will ask in my name, I will do it, that the Father
> may be glorified in the Son.
>
> (John 14:13 WEB)

When we ask for things, we receive them in order to bring God glory. I have to wonder if sometimes we don't get what we ask because it will not bring God the glory. We never know what impact what we want has on our lives. So, we must truly have faith in the One who knows our beginning, middle, and end.

Recently, God's been ministering to me about focus. Instead of being focused on the next big thing or what my main calling is in life, I am to focus on the present. What can I do today that will impact the kingdom of God? As the years go by, we will change geographical locations and we will change our abilities — thus our spheres of influence will change. Consequently, what God wants us to do will probably change. Your "calling" probably won't be one specific thing, rather you are called to be a follower of Jesus, which is a daily action of obedience to do whatever He puts in front of you. You will find yourself having multiple callings as you go through life. I'm called to be a daughter to my parents (which might entail caring for them as they age), I'm a sister, I'm called to be an aunt (Which is awesome — it's like being a friend and the fun parent without the responsibility) and I'm called to be a wife, which is a privilege — God literally entrusted one of his sons to me. I am to be a helper; I am to love and care for him, help him fight spiritual battles, be his prayer partner for life, and accountability buddy. I am called into kitchen ministry at my church. We all have many callings. Our success in how we walk them out is determined by whether or not we exemplify Christ in all of them. Sometimes they will fit into the boxes we've labeled ministry and other times they won't.

Ask God how He wants to use you today. Be willing to be used in any way, no matter how big or small.

What is the second type of Sword?

_____

Worship has the ability to _____Into focusing on _____.

Praise changes _____

God remains the _____. It is our _____that changes.

"And ye shall _____ the LORD your God, and he shall _____ thy bread, and thy water; and I will take _____ away from the midst of thee." Exodus 23:25 (KJV)

What different callings do you have?

_____

_____

How can you show forth Christ more in these callings?

_____

_____

_____

_____

MY LIPS SHALL PRAISE

But you are holy, you who inhabit the praises (tehillah) of Israel.

(Psa. 22:3 WEB)

"I just wish God would show up." I'm willing to bet you've said that yourself or heard someone say it. Well, the praises of His people is where He abides. We must first ask "What is praise?" Typically, praise and worship get lumped together but they are different. There are about 6 different Hebrew words that get translated into our one word, "praise".

First, we have "halal" — This is where we get the word hallelujah. It means to show, boast, to celebrate. Such praise is called upon in the sanctuary especially in times of festivals. It reminds me of the song "Look What The Lord Has Done," or "My God is awesome. He can move mountains. Keep me in the valley. Hide me from the rain." It's all boasting in the Lord. We can also boast in the Lord in speech, not just song, by testifying of what He has done in our life.

Second is "zamar" — It means to touch the strings or parts of a musical instrument and make music. This also refers to singing with music. There are some denominations that believe instruments are not to be used in praise and worship. This word is proof that they were intended to be. One of the words for praise literally means "with an instrument".

Thirdly, "yahdah" — this one is used 114 times in the Hebrew Bible. It means to use or hold out the hand, to revere or worship with extended hands. "Yahdah" is a recital of, and thanksgiving for Yahweh's mighty acts of salvation". Ever wonder if raising hands is biblical? It sure is! In fact, it's the most used form of praise. I really like Strong's definition because it says, "thanksgiving for Yahweh's mighty acts of salvation". It is good to praise God for salvation. Jesus even said in Luke 10:20 WEB "Nevertheless, don't rejoice in this, that the spirits are subject to you, but rejoice that your names are written in heaven:"

Lastly, "tehillah" — Laudation, glory, praise, song of praise worthy deeds, as in praising God for his attributes, where His glory is publicly displayed.

With all these definitions it's clear to see that praise must come from a heart that is humble. Knowing that one must decrease so the Lord can increase; accepting the gift of forgiveness and salvation. Recognizing how awesome God is and how great His love is toward you. I constantly ask God to give me a greater revelation and a holy awe of who He is. With greater revelation of God comes greater praise, which brings more of His presence, which brings more revelation and creates a beautiful ongoing circle of spiritual growth. If we are connecting all the dots: praise brings presence, presence brings joy, and joy brings praise.

> You will show me the path of life. In your presence is fullness of joy. In your right hand there are pleasures forever more.
>
> (Psa. 16:11 WEB)

> And be not drunk with wine, wherein is excess; but be filled with the Spirit; Speaking to yourselves in psalms and hymns and spiritual songs, singing and making melody in your heart to the Lord; Giving thanks always for all things unto God and the Father in the name of our Lord Jesus Christ;
>
> (Ephesians 5:18-20 KJV)

I want to note that it says, "yourselves" not "to one another". I looked up the original Greek translation and it is a reflexive pronoun. Meaning its reflecting on the subject, being you. Minister to <u>yourself</u> by singing hymns which are melodic words, and psalms, words with musical accompaniment, and spiritual songs. Spiritual songs are the "new songs" that the Spirit gives you. Sometimes it's just a tune or a hum. Or it can be words. The Spirit moves in different ways. You can also sing "old" songs; songs that you know that glorify Him, that speak to your heart and bring you a greater realization of His love and grace. Make praise a regular part of your day. There are so many good verses on singing. I want you to google "Bible verses on singing" and just soak it all in.

Here are some of my favorite verses on singing …

> But I will sing of your strength. Yes, I will sing aloud of your loving kindness in the morning. For you have been my high tower, a refuge in the day of my distress.

> To you, my strength, I will sing praises. For God is my high tower, the God of my mercy.
>
> (Psalm 59:16-17 WEB)

"And be not drunk with wine, wherein is excess; but be filled with the _____ Speaking to _____ in psalms and hymns and spiritual songs, singing and making melody in your heart to the Lord; Giving _____always for _____ things unto God and the Father in the name of our Lord Jesus Christ;" Ephesians 5:18-20 (KJV)

He _____ the praises of His people.

"You will show me the path of life. In your _____, there is fullness of _____. In your right hand there are pleasures forever more." Psa. 16:11 (WEB)

Where is God? _____

RECONFIGURING

In everything give thanks, for this is the will of God in Christ
Jesus toward you.

(1 Thessalonians 5:18 WEB)

Finally, brothers, whatever things are true, whatever things are
honorable, whatever things are just, whatever things are pure,
whatever things are lovely, whatever things are of good report:
if there is any virtue and if there is any praise, think about these
things.

(Philippians 4:8 WEB)

Consider this quote by Charles Swindol:

"The longer I live, the more I realize the impact of attitude on life.
Attitude, to me, is more important than facts. It is more important
than success, than what other people think or say or do. It is more
important than appearance, giftedness or skill. It will make or
break a company … a church … a home. The remarkable thing is
we have a choice every day regarding the attitude we will embrace
for that day."

We cannot change our past. We cannot change the fact that people will act in a certain way.
We cannot change the inevitable. The only thing we can do is play on the one string we have, and
that is our attitude. I am convinced that life is 10% what happens to me and 90% how I react to
it — and so it is with you. We are in charge of our attitudes. We are instructed in Philippians to
control our thoughts which in turn control our attitude.

You might not be able to change your circumstances, but by praising the Lord you can change
your attitude. You can be the thermostat, not the thermometer. This means you control the

atmosphere around you. You aren't a reflection of that atmosphere — you control your attitude. We all know someone who is just never happy. The world calls them pessimists. If you're being honest, you find it hard to be around those people. Guess what, calling yourself a pessimist is just an excuse not to work to be thankful and positive. As a child of God, you are called to give thanks in all, yes *all*, circumstances. God didn't say give thanks for all circumstances but *in* all circumstances. There is always something we can be thankful for. You waive the right to label yourself as a pessimist. I hear you all now, "You don't know my life. You don't know what I go through." I don't have to. Whatever has happened, Jesus' blood covered it. Whatever is going on, you have the victory in Jesus' name. Whatever will happen He'll walk you through it — *if* you lean on and trust Him with everything. Faith requires that you believe whole heartedly; that you do not waiver or doubt. By thinking, "I'm going to believe for this, but it probably won't happen so when it doesn't I'll just do this." Is horrible! That's a wish, not a faith filled request and God doesn't grant wishes. I do believe the reason for the many miracles in third world countries is because they literally have no other way. It's either God comes through, or they die. Do we have that kind of faith?

I want you to say one positive thing or give thanks for one thing in your life every hour today. It could be, "Lord, thank you for this coffee." "Thank you that my kid isn't screaming as I walk through this grocery store." "I have been blessed with a good job." Anything. Be creative. In all things give thanks.

Write a list of things you are thankful for. Feel free to get creative and make a word picture in this blank space.

WALKING THROUGH DARKNESS

From the end of the earth, I will call to you when my heart is
overwhelmed. Lead me to the rock that is higher than I.

(Psalm 61:2 WEB)

Do we always walk in the light? Are we always thinking positive? No. Sometimes we feel discouraged, our spirits are off balance. We can't live in this world without experiencing dark times. God knows that and offers us help with it. Do not give up when you feel nothing is going right, when you feel overwhelmed. When your dreams are on hold, or you think God is silent. We all have these thoughts and doubts, but we must refuse to stay in these thought patterns. It is in these times we must exercise our faith. We can choose to see these times as times of opportunity. Opportunities for growth, a spiritual check, redirection, strengthening of our faith, and healing. Take any negative thought captive before the Lord. Place the issue at the feet of Jesus seated at the throne. After you've recognized the dark circumstance or thought and surrendered it to God open your mouth and begin to change the atmosphere with praise. If you aren't to the point of singing out loud yet, then at least listen to worship music. Separate yourself from the world and pray. This is the journey to the Rock that is higher than us.

It's all about changing your focus from the problem to the problem solver. I can choose to dwell on an issue or occurrence, but this would be worry and it would only serve to magnify my problem. Instead, release and move forward. Have faith that when you placed your issue before God that He took it and is going to help you with it. Whenever it comes up in your mind again take that thought back to God and pray something to the effect of, "Lord, I thank you that you have control of _____ and even now you are resolving it and working it out for my good. If there's anything you need me to do, convict me of it."

Sometimes when I feel blue, I don't feel very spiritual. I know I am supposed to praise but I don't feel very enthusiastic. I desire to have a zeal and passion, but where does it come from? The intensity of your worship will be born from the awareness of where God has brought you from and the revelation of where He is taking you. It is sometimes helpful to keep a journal or record of what God has done in your life. It could be a small thing or a big thing. These occurrences are helpful to look back on when in times of darkness and silence. They serve as reminders of what God has done and strengthens your faith that God can do it again.

I don't have a radical amazing testimony of how I overcame addiction or how God rescued me from abuse. I never strayed far into the depths of sin and had to be pulled back (thank you, Jesus!). Many times, because of this, it was hard to find a passionate awareness of where God has brought me from. Personally, it is being aware that God has protected me from many unseen things that causes me to praise. It's the realization that only by His grace am I in the situation I'm in right now. There is always something you can praise God for. Even if it's as simple as thanking Him for letting you drive home without getting in an accident. I ask God every day to give me a revelation of His grace. To recognize all that He has done for me, that I might not take anything for granted. Thankfulness breeds a heart of praise.

I love this quote from Tony Miller, "You are a testimony to God's sustaining power. Many others have not survived your testimony."

That is a reason to praise! Many others have not survived what you have. You are an overcomer! By the grace of God, you have survived this world so far. Rejoice! "You are a testimony to God's sustaining power." That means your life could be the tool God uses to help others make it through difficult times. You can be an example to others if you let God work in and through you to make all things good. It starts with a heart surrendered.

A heart of gratitude births a heart of praise.

> You will have a song, as in the night when a holy feast is kept,
> and gladness of heart, as when one goes with a flute to come to
> Yahweh's mountain, to Israel's Rock.
>
> (Isaiah 30:29 WEB)

Then, this scripture takes an interesting turn going back to praising in the battle and the power of praise.

> "Yahweh will cause his glorious voice to be heard, and will show the
> descent of his arm, with the indignation of his anger, and the flame
> of a devouring fire, with a blast, storm, and hailstones. For through
> Yahweh's voice the Assyrian will be dismayed. He will strike him
> with his rod. Every stroke of the rod of punishment, which Yahweh
> will lay on him, will be with the sound of tambourines and harps.
> He will fight with them in battles, brandishing weapons."
>
> (Isaiah 30:30-32 WEB)

When we fight spiritual battles, it helps to have worship music filling the atmosphere. We fight to the tune of praise. God did it, should we not follow His example? Times of darkness or not having spiritual connectedness can sometimes be caused by what we have let into our minds as well as our dwelling. If we leave a small crack in any opening the enemy will find it. I believe this is the cause of a lot of nightmares and spirits of fear of the dark and such. We have the power to change this. When fighting against demonic presence in a house I find it helpful to have worship music playing. I have personally heard the testimonies of people who felt a better peace in their home after cleansing it and reclaiming their house for the Lord. When I say "cleansing" I'm not talking about any weird ritual or burning incense, I'm simply talking about taking spiritual authority over your house and commanding any forces of darkness to leave in the name of Jesus. Fill the air with worship, rid it of unclean things, proclaim Joshua 24:15 KJV" … but as for me and my house we will serve the Lord." Take action. Your house (and you) belong to God and anything not of God does not belong there. Just as we ask God to cleanse our hearts from any impurities we must also pray over our house. Ask Him to reveal any images, objects, or music that is not conducive to His presence and after He reveals them get rid of them. His presence is light. If we are in His presence, darkness cannot exist. Worship is the gateway to His presence. It is how we communicate in the spirit. We must worship Him in spirit and in truth.

My pastor recently said, "You cannot be light in this world unless you are in the light."

Change your focus from the _____ to the _____

The intensity of your worship is born from _____ of where God has brought you _____ and the revelation of _____ He is taking you.

"You are a testimony to God's sustaining power. Many others have not survived your testimony." -Tony Miller

Where can light be found? _____

Where can we find His presence? _____

BONUS CHAPTER!

Fit to Run the Race

Whether therefore you eat, or drink, or whatever you do, do all
to the glory of God.

(1 Corinthians 10:31 WEB)

We ask God to bless our food, but are we worshiping God by what we're eating? I have to wonder if there's a connection between the food and the taking away of sickness. The Lord warns many times in the Bible about gluttony and the sin that it is. If our lives are worshiping the Lord, we should be worshiping with what we choose to put into our body, since our body is the temple of the Holy Spirit. Many of our sicknesses would be taken away by eating right and not overeating. I know this is very hard for some, but eating can be a form of bondage. Even not eating enough healthy food can be detrimental. I once struggled with eating. I was in denial. I would calculate everything that went into my mouth. I was eating but I wasn't eating a balanced diet. I spent every hour of my day working out, planning what I would eat, making it, and eating it. Yes, I got my body fat down, but it was so low that I messed up my hormones and had health repercussions. The enemy will use any tactic he can to get you to be unhealthy. We are made in God's image which the enemy hates, so he will try to destroy us in any way possible. If you struggle with what to eat, bring it to the Lord. Ask for wisdom. Ask how you can glorify him with what you eat. Self-control is one of the fruits of the Spirit. He will cultivate it within you. Just seek Him and ask.

Whether you _____ or _____ do it _____ for the glory of God.

CHAPTER 3
THE SHIELD

THE SHIELD OF FAITH

> Above all, taking up the shield of faith, with which you will be
> able to quench all the fiery darts of the evil one.
>
> (Ephesians 6:16 WEB)

We, as disciples, are given weapons and tools to help us fight the "good fight". One of these tools is our Shield of Faith. In one scene, Wonder Woman arrives at a battlefield called No Man's Land. No one has been able to make any progress against the enemy for days. They've just been hiding in a fox hole, staying low to avoid the bullets of the enemy. Wonder Woman sees the need of the people. She knows she must do something. She takes off her cloche and begins to run through the battlefield behind her shield, drawing all the enemy fire. The good guys are able to sneak past and make headway against the enemy — saving the town. Her shield is keeping her safe. She's not peeking above it to determine the safest route, she's running behind it, trusting that it will protect her from what the enemy is throwing at her. Faith is our shield. Faith is how we extinguish the flaming arrows of the evil one. In Paul's days, flaming arrows were common knowledge. The defense against them was to soak the leather wrapped shields with water so when the arrows hit they would go out. We need to keep our shields wet by the water of the Word. We must become saturated with it in order to have a proper defense.

> That he might sanctify it, having cleansed it by the washing of
> water with the word.
>
> (Ephesians 5:26 WEB)

> So faith comes by hearing, and hearing by the word of God.
>
> (Romans 10:17 WEB)

If faith comes by hearing and hearing by the Word, then faith is built by the Word of God. The word for "Word" in both verses is rhema. So, this is the spoken Word of God. This word comes from fellowship; conversing with Him. Logos is the Bible, the written word. Rhema word of God can come to you while reading the Logos word. It is that moment when suddenly the scriptures come alive and seem to speak to you in your current situation. It's that "aha!" moment. The rhema word can also come to you in the car, in the shower, while you're cooking … really anywhere.

We need to have Faith and run behind it. Faith is what gets us from point A to point B or victory to victory.

> For we walk by faith, not by sight.
>
> (2 Corinthians 5:7 WEB)

What do we have faith in? What is this faith that we can run behind? It is the faith that God is who He says He is; that His word is true and that His promises are sure — that we are saved and redeemed. The following verses talk about the different forms of shields that are available to us as believers.

> You have also given me the shield of your salvation. Your right
> hand sustains me. Your gentleness has made me great.
>
> (Psalm 18:35 WEB)

Salvation is a great shield! It's literally Jesus blood over us like the blood over the doorposts of the Israelites that says "this house is protected." Fun fact, Believers covered by the blood cannot be possessed by evil spirits. They can be oppressed but the enemy can never actually take them over.

Then we see the Lord as a shield:

> He lays up sound wisdom for the upright. He is a shield to those
> who walk in integrity.
>
> (Proverbs 2:7 WEB)

"To those who walk in integrity." What does that mean? Webster's dictionary defines integrity as, "firm adherence to a code of especially moral artistic values: incorruptibility. An unimpaired condition: soundness. The state of being complete or undivided." If you are a woman of integrity that means you are following the code, the guidelines laid out in scripture; you have a sound mind, which comes from knowing who and whose you are. You are complete and undivided. You do not waiver. You do not say one thing and then the other. You are not hypocritical. You believe all of God's word and not just the parts you like. When we walk by faith it should be evident by our talk as well as our walk. Are we speaking God's word into our situation? Do we respond to problems based on *our* ability to fix them or do we respond based on God's ability to work it out?

Every day we are going to come up upon a battlefield, a decision. Many times throughout the Bible, God tells His people to do incredible tasks: build a wall, build an ark, tell pharaoh to release his whole work force, go before the king even though you could be killed, and so on. The subjects of these stories had to make the choice whether to walk by what they saw and perceived the situation to be, or to walk by what God told them to do, thus walking by faith.

"You will walk through fire, but not be burned."

Shadrach, Meshach, and Abednego had a choice to make. Do they walk by faith that God will take care of them or do they walk by what they see which is fire and death? Notice their verbiage in this passage.

> Shadrach, Meshach, and Abednego answered the king, "Nebuchadnezzar, we have no need to answer you in this matter. If it happens, our God whom we serve is able to deliver us from the burning fiery furnace; and he will deliver us out of your hand, O king. But if not, let it be known to you, O king, that we will not serve your gods or worship the golden image which you have set up.
>
> (Daniel 3:16-18 WEB)

They had Faith that God was capable of delivering them, but even if He didn't, they still would not disobey Him. They didn't have a word from God prior to this, saying that they'd be delivered. I believe if they had, they wouldn't have said, "even if." They would have left it at "our God is able to deliver us." In this story they knew God and the power He has. We have the knowledge and the promise! Our obedience should not be conditional on what God does for us. We obey and serve because He is worthy. He is Lord no matter what He does or doesn't do. Our faith should be firmly rooted in the word of God. Faith comes through blind obedience to God. You don't know how it's going to happen, but God said it so you're going to do it. God's word is true and whatever He says will come to pass.

If God told you to do it, He will see you through it.

What gets us from point A to point B? _____

2 Corinthians 5:7 (WEB) "for we walk by _____ and not by _____."

What faith do we walk by?

_____

Our obedience should not be _____ on what_____.

If _____to do it, _____.

Ephesians 6:16 (WEB) "Above all, lift up the [protective] shield of _____with which you can _____all the flaming arrows of the_____."

Where does faith come from?

_____

What Word is faith built by? _____

Do we make decisions based on what we perceive the situation to be or by what God has said it would be?

WHAT IS FAITH

I had finished writing this segment when, in my own personal study, I found myself in Hebrews 11. I decided I had to come back and add a little more. I suggest you read Hebrews 11 in its entirety on your own, but I will highlight some of the main verses here. Let's start with verse 1.

> Now faith is assurance of things hoped for, proof of things not seen.
>
> (Hebrews 11:1 WEB)

The amplified adds that faith is "the title deed". Which to me makes a lot more sense. Imagine if you will, I live in Colorado and someone gives me a deed to a piece of land in Tennessee in my name. I know it exists and that it belongs to me. I can't see it because I'm on the other side of the country. I'm not sure how I'm going to get there. I didn't do anything to earn it, but it's mine. I hold the title deed. If you read the all of Hebrews 11 you'll see it's filled with examples of God showing up and handing His people "title deeds". God is the author of time and space. What we need exists somewhere or at some time in our future. We don't see the breakthrough, but God sees it and has sent it. He invites us to be able to see it too through eyes of faith. It's important to note that faith is not confidence that what we hope for will come true. It is the confidence that what God has said will come to pass.

Hebrews 12:2 tells us that Jesus is the author and finisher of our faith. That means He authors our faith, what we hope for, and brings it to completion. He writes the title deed and gives it to us. We then can have faith that it is real and will come to fruition. Often, we are trying to be the author of our faith. We're trying to write our own title deeds to stuff, then trying to claim the property when we don't have that authority. Then, we get mad at God when what we hope for doesn't come to pass. We ask, "well didn't you say if I only had faith like a mustard seed, I could do anything?" Even Jesus only did what the Father did.

> Jesus therefore answered them, "Most certainly, I tell you, the Son can do nothing of himself, but what he sees the Father doing. For whatever things he does, these the Son also does likewise.
>
> (John 5:19 WEB)

We have to look and see what God is up to. That way we can see what His plan is and come beside Him with faith in what He's going to do. We are called to co-labor with Christ; to work with Him. If the Lord has given you a promise you can have faith that it will come to pass.

Now faith is also the assurance of things we don't see. Faith is what makes us able to say God exists. We can't physically see Him, but by faith we know He's real.

> Without faith it is impossible to be well pleasing to him, for he who comes to God must believe that he exists, and that he is a rewarder of those who seek him.
>
> (Hebrews 11:6 WEB)

You must have faith that He is a good father and rewards those who seek Him. This also means you have to earnestly seek Him, which is to obey.

Faith is _____ in what we hope for and _____ about what we do not see.

Faith is not _____.

Jesus is the _____ and _____ of our faith.

We can do _____ apart from the Father.

Without _____ it is impossible to please God.

Anyone who comes to God (in prayer) Must first believe that He _____

And rewards those that_____

FAITHFULLY OBEYING

For as the body apart from the spirit is dead, even so faith apart
from works is dead.

(James 2:26 WEB)

Wasn't Abraham our father justified by works, in that he offered
up Isaac his son on the altar? You see that faith worked with his
works, and by works faith was perfected. So the scripture was
fulfilled which says, "Abraham believed God, and it was accounted
to him as righteousness," and he was called the friend of God. You
see then that by works, a man is justified, and not only by faith. In
the same way, wasn't Rahab the prostitute also justified by works,
in that she received the messengers and sent them out another way?
For as the body apart from the spirit is dead, even so faith apart
from works is dead.

(James 2:21-26 WEB)

We are not made righteous and justified by our works or acts of obedience, but by our faith. If we
have faith in God and His word it should be evident by our acts. Jesus said you will know a tree
by its fruit. You should be able to recognize a believer by their fruit; their words and actions. If no
one ever had any fruits of the spirit in their life — love, joy, peace, patience kindness, gentleness,
and self control — would you be able to say they had the holy spirit?

Your act of obedience can be a way to witness to others. Shadrach, Meshach, and Abednego's
obedience showed a living God to a king, and then to a whole nation. They could have easily said,
"Now that we've obeyed God and did not bow down to idols what do we get in return? To be
thrown into the furnace?!" But instead they chose the act of faith and obedience. They chose to obey
even when it would cost them their lives. They didn't know going into the furnace that God would
show up. I'm sure they were thinking, "We are going to become martyrs," but they would have
become martyrs gladly. Will we obey only when it's convenient or will we obey no matter the cost?

We fight on spiritual battlegrounds. These battlegrounds are places in our lives or in the lives of those around us that the enemy has placed strong holds. He's spoken lies in your finances. One of the most common one lies is, "You don't have enough to tithe. Surely that must not be what God wants you to do." — even though you know that God desires a cheerful giver. We're then given the choice whether to agree with that outlook and say, "yes, it is looking rather slim", or act out of obedience, pick up our shield of faith and run behind the promise that God will provide our needs if we obey Him. By going the faith route we have conquered that battlefield and won the victory.

Another example that I've personally warred with is the following lie — because in human eyes, it's a true statement. "I am not qualified to do this job, there are others that would be better, that are better. Surely you do not want me for this task." Any time we rely on our own strength we do not need faith. We cannot be effective witnesses if we only do things by our strength. Doing things on our own brings glory to self. When people see you do something anyone can do, they don't see the difference that Christ is making. However, when you allow God to work through you to do something extraordinary that requires all your faith, people will see the great thing Christ is doing and thus see Christ in you. That is why it is important to give testimony of what God has done in your life: to speak of his goodness openly, to be transparent so others can see what faith in Jesus can accomplish. It's not about elevating yourself, but elevating God — giving Him the glory in all things. Every good idea you've had, He placed it there. Every skill set you have, He created. Yes, we can and should cultivate these gifts, but don't forget, He created them.

I will obey …
(Circle one)

  a. When it's convenient
  b. If it feels right
  c. No matter the cost
  d. If I know it will end well

"For just as the [human] body without the spirit is dead, so_____ without _____ [of _____ is also _____." James 2:26 WEB

What are some battle grounds you fight on?

_____
_____

What promises in scripture can you find to battle with?

_____
_____

We cannot be _____
_____if we only do things by _____
_____.

Joyce Meyers once said, "Faith is not always to keep us from having trouble, it is to carry us through trouble."

PRACTICING FAITH

… but the righteous will live by his faith.

(Habakkuk 2:4 WEB)

The AMPC version further expounds like this, "the rigidly just and the uncompromisingly righteous". What does being uncompromisingly righteous mean? Don't let that movie in your house, don't let that angry word be uttered. Know when to speak and when to hold your tongue. Do not be swayed by outside influences, but rather be led by the prompting of the Spirit and the word of God. I want to highlight this word "rigid". In karate we have a hand technique called shuto, meaning "knife hand". When teaching this technique, I am always sternly reminding my students, "hands rigid!" It takes a constant effort to not curve the hands and not have fingers splayed out. The reason we do this is so when we go to break boards or an attacker's grip, they break, and we do not. The enemy is strong. If we strike with a weak technique because we weren't rigid, we will get hurt and the enemy will remain standing.

Be rigid. Be uncompromising.

For therein is the righteousness of God revealed from faith to faith:
as it is written, The just shall live by faith.

(Romans 1:17 KJV)

Here the Bible says from faith to faith. Once you see a method work, you're going to use it more often, you will become stronger at it, and it will be second nature. Your faith will lead to more faith. The more you use it, the more results you will see and the more you will want to use it.

I had this happen to me for the first time one day when I went to work. One of my co workers was having a lot of pain in her leg. I felt an urge by the Spirit to pray for her. There we were in the broom closet speaking healing into that leg. After we said amen, I went about working. A few moments later I saw her and she was in tears because she had no more pain. This grew my faith drastically and it made me want to start testing this prayer concept on more things. We always hear we have not because we ask not. It's like the other saying, you miss one-hundred percent of the shots you don't take. You'll never know what can be accomplished through prayer if you never pray.

I would like you to do a couple of things. Write down at least three things you're specifically praying for. Eventually, you will receive answers to these and it will be a testimony of God answering your prayer. Seeing these answers will be an encouragement to you that will spur you on to use your faith more — and remember, sometimes God's answers don't look like what we had in mind. Make sure you're bringing your problems to Him and waiting on His solutions, not just asking Him for your idea of a solution. A lot of times we pray for answers, but prayer isn't about making your will a reality. God's ways are higher than ours and He knows what is best for us. Trust Him with whatever is on your heart — His answer might not make any sense to us at the time, but we must continue to have faith that God is working all things out for our good.

Test out your faith. God gave you the Holy Spirit. Are you utilizing it? Ask someone today how you can pray for them. Ask the Holy Spirit who you should intercede for in your time of prayer.

I experienced an awesome connection with the Holy Spirit while praying one day. As I was going through my morning prayer, my friend popped into my mind. I added her into my prayer. An hour later I realized that it was the day she started a new job and probably needed someone to intercede for her for strength and confidence. The Holy Spirit knew she needed encouragement, so He moved me to pray for her. God gives us the opportunity to co-labor with Him to accomplish His plans and purposes here on earth to bless us and others in the process. We are spiritual beings with the ability to operate in the spirit. When we pray we are operating in the spirit realm. Through faith in Jesus, we have authority in the spirit realm, connection to the Holy Spirit who guides our words, and the right to call on the name of Jesus! Will we take up our shield of faith and run behind it?

To close this section on faith, I will leave you with one of my favorite verses.

> For by you, I advance through a troop. By my God, I leap over a wall.
>
> (Psalm 18:29 WEB)

The _____ will live by his _____-

Be _____

Be _____

Romans 1:17 (KJV) "For therein is the _____ of God revealed from _____ to faith: as it is written, The _____ shall live by faith"

The more _____ you use, the more _____ you will see.

The more you _____your faith.

Write down at least 3 areas of your life that you will pray for and seek Gods answer to.

_____

_____

_____

Who am I going to pray for?_____

FAITH IN USE

> You ask, and don't receive, because you ask with wrong motives,
> so that you may spend it on your pleasures.
>
> (James 4:3 WEB)

A lot of us have been misguided by the "name it and claim it" principle. You know — the one where if you want a new car or a better house you just specifically pray for that certain make and model until you get it ... and if you don't receive it, it's because you didn't have enough faith. We're told so many times that we don't have because we do not ask. But we're never given the rest of the verse. Our asking must be in line with God's will and purpose. Like the verse says, we ask and do not receive because we ask with wrong motives. There are certain things we know are in His will because He has said so in His word. For example, 1 Timothy 2:4 WEB, "who desires all people to be saved and come to full knowledge of the truth."

It is God's will that all should be saved. So we can know that when we pray for the salvation of others we are in God's will and can have faith that it will come to pass. Praying for others salvation is something we need to be doing.

> I exhort therefore, first of all, that petitions, prayers, intercessions,
> and givings of thanks be made for all men: for kings and all who
> are in high places, that we may lead a tranquil and quiet life in
> all godliness and reverence. For this is good and acceptable in the
> sight of God our Savior, who desires all people to be saved and
> come to full knowledge of the truth.
>
> (1 Timothy 2:1-4 WEB)

What should be made for all people? _____

What grouping of people does it specifically say to pray for?

_____

What should we pray for them for?

This is good and pleasing in the sight of God. I always like knowing going into something that God is going to be pleased with the outcome. It's like being given the recipe to your mom's favorite dessert. You know she's going to be happy with it, so it's worth doing. To tie this in with our verse in James, consider this: we don't have godly government — we don't have leaders that are godly and dignified in every way. Have we prayed for them? Or have we just complained about how horrible they are?

We know and can have faith that if we pray, God will answer because we know by His word that this is His will — for us to be intercessors. We are the warriors on this battleground. He'll send us reinforcements, give us supplies, energy, food, weapons, but we are the feet on the ground. Take up your shield of faith and wage war against the gates of Hell.

LOADING ...

Loading ... We've all been at the computer screen just waiting on all the signals to connect so we can get to where we want. Quite frankly, this is often a great picture of our faith. We have faith that eventually the page will come up. We really don't understand what the computer is doing or all the little mechanisms and signals that are firing to bring us to the picture we want to see on the screen, but do we really care? Most likely not. We just want to know that when we click on something the desired effect will happen. I feel like this is how we view our prayers. We need to understand that there are many factors to receiving an answer in prayer.

First, there's your heart. Are you in a right place with God? Is there anything hindering you from direct contact? We discussed this in the introduction. Is your computer hooked to the internet? If you don't have signal nothing is going to load.

Secondly, there may be a battle in the spirit hindering your answer from getting to you. Some virus is blocking you from getting to your page! If we know that we are praying in God's will, we need to stand fast and not give up. Don't just hit the power button and close the screen.

We are given an example of when this happened to Daniel:

> Then he said to me, "Don't be afraid, Daniel; for from the first day that you set your heart to understand, and to humble yourself before your God, your words were heard. I have come for your words' sake. But the prince of the kingdom of Persia withstood me twenty-one days; but, behold, Michael, one of the chief princes, came to help me because I remained there with the kings of Persia.
>
> (Daniel 10:12-13 WEB)

Here we have Daniel — the moment he began praying and fasting his prayer was heard. It says that the prince of Persia opposed Gabriel the messenger for three weeks. Then Michael the chief priest steps in and Gabriel finally gets to Daniel. The demonic forces were trying to hinder the answer from the Lord. A lot is happening that we don't see. Your answer is on its way. That's where we must have faith, during the wait.

Thirdly; timing. It may not be God's timing. We ask and do not receive because it is not time for us to have what we are asking for. You may not be spiritually ready for it. You may not be physically ready. There may be something God is trying to teach you. In the hard times it's wise to ask God what He wants you to learn from the experience. Ask Him to show you what His will and purpose is for it and ask the Holy Spirit how you should pray.

Take aways:
There are many factors to seeing your answer to prayer.

First:_____

Second:_____
(spiritual oppostition)

Third:_____

In the same way, the Spirit also helps our weaknesses, for we don't know how to pray as we ought. But the Spirit himself makes intercession for us with groanings which can't be uttered. (Romans 8:26 WEB)

The Spirit _____ in our _____.

The Spirit _____for us.

CHAPTER 4

TRUTH

SANCTIFYING TRUTH

Sanctify them in your truth. Your word is truth. As you sent me into the world, even so I have sent them into the world. For their sakes I sanctify myself, that they themselves also may be sanctified in truth.

(John 17:17-19 WEB)

The logos word attesting to God is truth. The absolute truth, it sanctifies; "to set apart as or declare holy; consecrate."

The word (logos) became flesh.

(John 1:14 WEB)

In John 1:1 we see Jesus is the word: "In the beginning was the Word, and the Word was with God, and the Word was God." Logos means, "expressing the thoughts of the Father through the Spirit". Ever since the beginning, Jesus has been expressing the thoughts of the father through being linked with the Spirit to the world. He has been attesting to his greatness and goodness.

Truth (not merely truth as spoken; truth of idea, reality, sincerity, truth in the moral sphere, divine truth revealed to man, straightforwardness) became embodied in Jesus. Jesus is the divine truth revealed to man. Jesus solidified this truth in the book of John.

Jesus said to him, I am the way, the truth, and the life. No one comes to the Father, except through me.

(John 14:6 WEB)

Sin cannot stand in the presence of the Lord, thus to become one with the Father, Son, and Holy Spirit we would have to be sanctified. We know that by receiving and believing in Jesus that we are cleansed by His blood and made holy.

That he might sanctify it, having cleansed it by the washing of water with the word, that he might present the assembly to himself gloriously, not having spot or wrinkle or any such thing; but that it should be holy and without defect.

(Ephesians 5:26-27 WEB)

God chose you from the beginning for salvation through sanctification of the Spirit and belief in the truth.

(2 Thessalonians 2:13 WEB)

By which will we have been sanctified through the offering of the body of Jesus Christ once for all. ... For by one offering he has perfected forever those who are being sanctified.

(Hebrews 10:10, 14. WEB)

How much more will the blood of Christ, who through the eternal Spirit offered himself without defect to God, cleanse your conscience from dead works to serve the living God?

(Hebrews 9:14 WEB)

By this logic no one can come to the Father unless they go through the truth which is Jesus who is also the word, and the word is truth. Our job is to bring people to Jesus; bring them to truth. Lead them to the place where they can find truth. The truth of who God is and what He's done.

We're called to show people Jesus through words of love and truth, and through our testimony.

What sustains all things? _____

John 17:17 (WEB)- "Sanctify them in your _____, your _____ is truth"

Jesus is

The _____

The _____

The _____

What is the definition of logos?_____

SPEAKING TRUTH

> But speaking truth in love, we may grow up in all things into him
> who is the head, Christ.
>
> (Ephesians 4:15 WEB)

The word truth in the above verse is alētheúō (literally, "to truth") includes Spirit-led confrontation where it is vital to tell the truth so others can live in God's reality rather than personal illusion. There are times when we are called into some confrontational situations for the benefit of others so that they can live in the reality of who God is and who He created them to be. The key here is that we speak it in love.

> Brothers, even if a man is caught in some fault, you who are
> spiritual must restore such a one in a spirit of gentleness; looking
> to yourself so that you also aren't tempted. Bear one another's
> burdens, and so fulfill the law of Christ. For if a man thinks
> himself to be something when he is nothing, he deceives himself.
>
> (Galatians 6:1-3 WEB)

We have to be very careful when calling others out. First off, we are only supposed to do this to fellow believers; those who are seeking a right relationship with the Lord. Those who are not actively striving for this aren't going to care what you have to say, and it will end badly. We also can't come from a place of false superiority. We all have sinned and come short of the glory of God. Thus, one of us is not any better than the other. We don't point out someone else short comings to hide our own or to make ours look smaller. Any advice has to come from a spirit of wanting to see a person live the life God has for them to their fullest potential. It is not our responsibility to tell the world they are sinning. Trust me, they know. Not speaking the truth in love or with the grace of God is not helpful.

Within the body we should have someone who will help keep us spiritually accountable. Someone we can trust to call us out if they see something wrong in our actions. Likewise, in order to be this person for someone else you have to have a relationship with them. You can't just go around to random people calling them out. Small groups are great places to form relationships with fellow believers and encourage one another to walk in the ways of the Lord.

> With all lowliness and humility, with patience, bearing with one
> another in love.
>
> (Ephesians 4:2 WEB)

As far as the outside world goes, God is the judge. We show people His ways through our actions. We share the beauty of salvation and the grace and mercy of the Loving Father. When they finally come face to face with Him, they come face to face with the truth. This type of truth revelation brings people to repentance. God will reveal to them the err of their ways. We don't need to tell people what they are doing wrong. We need to tell them the truth in love which is God loves them and wants to clean the dirt and grime of the streets off them, adopt them and give them a new name — His name. There's an open invite for forgiveness. We sometimes want to make a person come to repentance faster, but we have to let God do this work in their life in His perfect timing.

How do we show God's truth to people? It comes from being authentic. From living out the truth. From looking like Jesus. From knowing the truth. Truly knowing and believing it. which only comes through study of the Word and prayer. To be able to speak the truth we must know the truth.

Be _____

Be _____

Be _____

_____ with one another in _____

Speak truth in _____

Our job is to _____.

THE TRUTH THAT SUPPORTS

Stand therefore, having your loins girt about with truth.
(Ephesians 6:14 KJV)

It is rather amusing to me that Paul chose a girdle to represent truth. Girdles help hold everything up. They are like a back brace. Truth is what sustains all things. It is the firm foundation our belief is built on.

We've looked at truth as a person, let's now look at it as a girdle. Keep in mind a girdle is something that helps you stand up right, like a brace. Truth will hold you up. When you're feeling down remind yourself of the truth of God's word: the truth of who you are in Him, the truth of His promises towards you, and the truth that He loves you immensely no matter what you've done. I encourage you to keep notes of what truths God has revealed to you to have handy in those down times. So that you can be reminded of the ways God has shown His love for you.

The word can defend you from spiritual attacks. One of our enemy's greatest tactics is deception, creating an illusion. He's used it since the beginning of time. We must know the truth of God's word to be able to discern a lie.

Here's an example for you: I was once a worship leader for the youth at a local church. One day I was practicing guitar and nothing was going right. My fingers would not go into position, I couldn't find the right key to sing in. I couldn't even play an interlude without the chords written down. I began to feel discouraged. Seemingly logical thoughts began to flood my brain. "You're not equipped to be a director of music. You don't have the skills to train young people. You don't even know this yourself. The church would be better off with someone more qualified."

Looking back these were lies of the devil. He likes to take tiny bits of what seems like logic and fashion them into hurdles and blockades to keep you from doing the will of God. Thankfully the Spirit began to come to my rescue and remind me of His truths. I was called for that position at that time. There were lives being touched by it. God didn't require perfection, He required obedience. I heard the spirit saying to me, "I have called you. Now return your focus to me, the truth, and walk in the position I placed you in.."

For it is God who works in you both to will and to work, for his good pleasure.

(Philippians 2:13 WEB)

And God is able to make all grace abound to you, that you, always having all sufficiency in everything, may abound to every good work.

(2 Corinthians 9:8 WEB)

If anyone speaks, let it be as it were the very words of God. If anyone serves, let it be as of the strength which God supplies, that in all things God may be glorified through Jesus Christ, to whom belong the glory and the dominion forever and ever. Amen.

(1 Peter 4:11 WEB)

The word can _____ from _____.

Why is it important to keep the word fresh on your mind?

_____

Write down some of your take aways from the verses.

_____
_____
_____
_____
_____

The word is truth. Seek to know the word so you will know it to be reminded of it.

You cannot be reminded of something you never experienced or read.

DISCERNING TRUTH

> Don't be conformed to this world, but be transformed by the
> renewing of your mind, so that you may prove what is the good,
> well-pleasing, and perfect will of God.
>
> (Romans 12:2 WEB)

In order to discern truth you need to be acquainted with it. The word is truth, it is living and active. Both the written word and the rhema word; the words spoken by the still small voice, when the Holy Spirit delivers a message to the heart. Romans 10:17 says, "so faith comes by hearing, and hearing by the (Rhema) word of God". True hearing comes by the still small voice of God. It is his voice that we need to become adapt at discerning.

The rhema word is God's words directly to you about your situation and your life. These are truths just for you. Faith, which is complete confidence and trust, comes through these truths. Our faith, our confidence in Christ, is made strong by personal revelation from God. Our faith is made strong by hearing His rhema word.

Always test things against the word of God. If a leader says something that doesn't sit right with your spirit put it up against the Word, which is truth. Does the statement line up with God's word? For example, someone says, "you cannot serve God and drink alcohol." Or "you can't be a believer and have a tattoo, if you eat pork, you're sinning … etc." be careful when people try to make salvation about works of the flesh instead of the saving power of God's word.

The word says,

> Go your way—eat your bread with joy, and drink your wine with
> a merry heart; for God has already accepted your works.
>
> (Ecclesiastes 9:7 WEB)

> And be not drunken with wine, wherein is riot, but be filled with
> the Spirit.
>
> (Ephesians 5:18 WEB)

You can have wine, but don't let it affect your judgement. Don't be drunk on wine that leads to debauchery (excessive indulgence in sensual pleasures) but rather be filled with the spirit as your source of Joy.

> All things are lawful for me," but not all things are profitable. "All
> things are lawful for me," but not all things build up.
> (1 Corinthians 10:23 WEB)

You have been set free from the bonds of religion and the old law that said if you ate or drank certain things you would be condemned. This verse stated that what you eat and drink is permissible, but it may not be helpful to you. You have to follow the Spirit's leading. Some things aren't salvation issues, but they certainly won't help you or edify you. Even though we are free from the law we still need to conduct ourselves in a manner that rightly shows forth Christ to others. Furthermore, Romans 14 points out that if a fellow believer has a personal conviction to abstain from eating or drinking something or believes certain days are sacred, we are to respect their personal convictions.

> Yet if because of food your brother is grieved, you walk no longer
> in love. Don't destroy with your food him for whom Christ died.
> (Romans 14:15 WEB)

> But he who doubts is condemned if he eats, because it isn't of faith;
> and whatever is not of faith is sin.
> (Romans 14:23 WEB)

We need to be careful that we do not try to be the voice of God in someone's life. We might be convicted that an action is approved by God but if our fellow believer is not convicted and has doubts that it is approved, he would be sinning if he partook in the activity. If someone asks you about your opinion on the matter, I do believe it is okay to share your personal convictions. Always make sure that you do not present a personal conviction or personal preference as a biblical absolute. And whatever you do walk in love.

> Only let your way of life be worthy of the Good News of Christ,
> that whether I come and see you or am absent, I may hear of your
> state, that you stand firm in one spirit, with one soul striving for
> the faith of the Good News.
> (Philippians 1:27 WEB)

For the law of the Spirit of life in Christ Jesus made me free from
the law of sin and of death.

(Romans 8:2 WEB)

That which enters into the mouth doesn't defile the man; but that
which proceeds out of the mouth, this defiles the man.

(Matthew 15:11 WEB)

Always seek things out for yourself. God loves to reveal His truths for those who seek them. He has hidden them like Easter eggs and takes great joy in watching you find them. Try doing an in-depth study on your favorite verse by looking up the original Greek or Hebrew and really expanding your knowledge of what God is saying. Experiencing truth starts by inviting the Holy Spirit to speak to you. It reminds me of when you have a friend and you complain how they never talk to you but you never message them. You wait for them to message you first. The Word says draw near to me and I will draw near to you. Send the message first. The Holy Spirit is a gentlemen and won't intrude and rule over you life. He wants to be invited. Before you read the word invite Him to speak to you. I'm not saying He'll never speak to you unless you speak first, I'm saying be careful to not become lazy in your relationship. Pursue this relationship with Him.

Gird yourself everyday with truth. Get up and read the Word. Listen to it in the car or while you are getting ready. Praying without ceasing is involving God in every part of your day, not having only certain times where you speak to Him, but having constant communication. When I began a relationship with my now husband, I don't think we ever said goodbye. Sure, there were times we had to drive, go to work, go to school, you know do life. but we never said goodbye. We just didn't answer the last text until we were able to. The conversation didn't end, it was merely on pause. It's been a 2.5 year ongoing conversation. You don't just call God once a day, you constantly talk to Him throughout the day. This is how we experience truth. The more we are in communication the more familiar we are to His voice and can hear it better. Which means we can discern truth better. Write it upon your heart, take it with you.

"Do not be _____to this world, but be _____ by the renewal of your _____, that by testing you may _____ what is the will of God, what is _____and _____ and perfect." (Romans 12:2 WEB)

"faith comes by _____, and hearing by the (Rhema) _____ of God". (Romans 10:17 WEB)

"Only let your _____ be _____ of the Good News of Christ, that whether I come and see you or am absent, I may _____ of your state, that you _____in one spirit, with one soul striving for the _____ of the Good News," (Philippians 1:27 WEB)

Our faith is made strong by

_____.

God loves to reveal His truth to who? _____

How can you put on the belt of truth today? _____

What are some truths that God has spoken in your life?

_____

_____

  If you can't think of any, ask God to reveal some to you.

TRUTH IN ACTION

> I have no greater joy than this: to hear about my children walking in truth.
>
> (3 John 4 WEB)

It's time we start following the Word and walking in the truth.

> My little children, let's not love in word only, or with the tongue only, but in deed and truth.
>
> (1 John 3:18 WEB)

This word "truth" in its original Greek is alétheia (al-ay'-thi-a). Sounds like a great name for a female warrior. Alaythia, guarder of truth — has a nice ring to it. Any way, it means not merely truth as spoken, but truth of idea, reality, sincerity, truth in the moral sphere, divine truth revealed to man, straightforwardness.

Here, it highlights the fact that we're to show people Jesus with action and truth. Truth of idea and reality; our reality should reflect a living Savior. We should be sincere with one another; not acting one way and feeling another. If you recall, that was the definition of integrity — the state of being complete or undivided. Truth in the moral sphere — Having morals, what we do when no one is looking, being true to the life which we were called. Again, not acting morally right then truly being morally abase.

Then, there's acting in divine truth revealed to man. Truly believing in who He says you are, what He did for you, and believing that you are redeemed — that you've been set free and house the Holy Spirit — and *then* acting based on this knowledge. Be straight forward about the truth. Don't water down the potency of the gospel and the amazingness of what God did! Be bold in your truth! No one likes a watered-down soda. People overseas don't even put ice in their soda for this reason. They think Americans are nuts. Don't sell Jesus short. Our verbiage and actions should reflect the truth of what He's done. We don't have to stress about trying to accomplish this on our own.

> However when he, the Spirit of truth, has come, he will guide you
> into all truth, for he will not speak from himself; but whatever he
> hears, he will speak. He will declare to you things that are coming.
> He will glorify me, for he will take from what is mine, and will
> declare it to you.
>
> (John 16:13-14 WEB)

The Holy Spirit will guide us in truth and help us to walk it out. The Spirit is how we receive that rhema word of truth. We must work on being in tune with the Spirit and ask God to move freely in our hearts and lives. We must ask Him to take away anything that hinders the Spirit from having full control.

And finally, Truth binds us together.

> The elder, to the chosen lady and her children, whom I love in
> truth, and not I only, but also all those who know the truth, for
> the truth's sake, which remains in us, and it will be with us forever.
>
> (2 John 1:1-2 WEB)

We're placing the emphasis on, "not I only, but also <u>all those who know the truth.</u>" We are all bound together by the universal truth of God. Not by social status, age, or race but by God's everlasting truth."

In your own words give a description of the forms of truth.

Truth of idea :

_____

Truth of reality :

_____

Truth in morals :

_____

Divine truth :

_____

Straightforwardness :

_____

Write a prayer expressing asking for discernment of what is truth and to tune your ear to the voice of God.

CHAPTER 5

LOVE

LOVE

Beloved, let's love one another, for love is of God; and everyone who loves has been born of God, and knows God. He who doesn't love doesn't know God, for God is love. By this God's love was revealed in us, that God has sent his one and only Son into the world that we might live through him. In this is love, not that we loved God, but that he loved us, and sent his Son as the atoning sacrifice for our sins. Beloved, if God loved us in this way, we also ought to love one another. No one has seen God at any time. If we love one another, God remains in us, and his love has been perfected in us. By this we know that we remain in him and he in us, because he has given us of his Spirit. We have seen and testify that the Father has sent the Son as the Savior of the world. Whoever confesses that Jesus is the Son of God, God remains in him, and he in God. We know and have believed the love which God has for us. God is love, and he who remains in love remains in God, and God remains in him. In this, love has been made perfect among us, that we may have boldness in the day of judgment, because as he is, even so we are in this world. There is no fear in love; but perfect love casts out fear, because fear has punishment. He who fears is not made perfect in love. We love him, because he first loved us. If a man says, "I love God," and hates his brother, he is a liar; for he who doesn't love his brother whom he has seen, how can he love God whom he has not seen? This commandment we have from him, that he who loves God should also love his brother.

(1 John 4:7-21 WEB)

Only love can save the world" - Wonder Woman

What a powerful statement that is given by someone of the world. They are so close to understanding the whole picture but are just missing a piece of the puzzle. A friend of mine told me, while talking about life and the meaning behind it, that life and our existence is about finding true love. Is she wrong? Not entirely. For the unbeliever ultimate love that everyone runs after is the intimate love between two people. We're in a culture that focuses on finding your true love — your prince charming — and sometimes they focus on just finding love for the moment. A love that doesn't even last and somehow they're ok with that! That is only one type of love and one that fails at that. We are told in John 4:7 that God is love. So yes, in a way, finding love is our quest — the world is just looking in all the wrong places.

If all that sounded pretty confusing it's probably because we use love for how we like pizza and we also use love for how we love our spouse. But those are two entirely different feelings. Let's go back real quick to the basics of love. In the New Testament there are different words used for love. We are going to look at three of those.

Agapae:

Which is the plural of agape. It means love-feasts; also translated "feasts of charity". These are essentially dinners where the poorer Christians and the wealthy Christians ate together to bring about and encourage mutual relationships e. These feasts were often funded by the wealthier Christians. In the new testament church everyone brought what they had and shared it. This word can be found in Jude 1:12, 2 Peter 2:13, 1 Corinthians 11:17 the concept is found in acts 2:42, Acts 20:7. The observance of love feasts seemed to have disappeared around 200 ad.

Philia:

This love is one of a dear friend. This love comes from relationship; doing life with someone.

Agape:

It is God's countenance towards mankind and believers of Jesus especially. It is His will that His children have this love toward one another because agape expresses His nature, and He wants His children to represent Him. Love is seen by the actions that are birthed from it. For example, when God sent His son Jesus, it was an action that was the result of His Agape love for us. This love does not come from the worthiness of whom it is shown towards. Humans are not worthy of the love God has for us. It was a choice by God for seemingly no reason. God had a reason but to the minds of humans it makes no sense. Christian love centers on obedience to God's commands.

Thus, self-will that is self-pleasing is the antithesis of love for God / agape love. Christian love goes against the norm. It doesn't come from a flesh feeling or impulse nor is it directed towards someone you'd have a natural inclination to love, but rather from the Spirit. "It expresses the deep and constant love and interest of a perfect being towards entirely unworthy objects."- Strong's Greek dictionary of the New Testament.

All the words for love used in the passage in 1 John 4 are translated from agape love. In order to have agape love for one another you have to be in God and filled with His spirit, thus able to have the fruit of the spirit, love. Agape love has its source in God and I believe it is impossible for humans to have this love for one another without being connected to God. The love that the world knows is a conditional love. Even the love you have for your parents comes from the fact that they formed bonds with you as you grew up. You were conditioned to love them. Love comes from God. If you don't love, you do not know God, because God is love. He showed us the proof of His love through sending His son. This act of love is what will save the world. Since God is love let's put the word "God" in the place of "love" in the quote from the first section.

> "Now I know that only God can save this world ... so I stay,
> I fight, and I give ... for the world I know can be. This is my
> mission, now. Forever."
>
> -Wonder Woman

We know that only God can save the world. So, we stay, we fight, we give because we know the promises of the Lord. We know what He has instructed us to do. We will fight for love and fight to see His kingdom come. We are the warriors that will take the ground. We will fight back the forces of darkness and hatred in the power of the Holy Spirit. We will fight for the world we know can be that was revealed to us by the word. His Kingdom come on Earth as it is in Heaven. This is our mission.

Wonder Woman fights for the world she knows could be. This is a statement of faith. She sees mankind's potential, the good that lies within and fights to bring it out. We, as Christians, are to see people the way God sees them. Through the eyes of love. The greatest commandment is to love the Lord your God with all your heart, soul, and might and the second is like it, love your neighbor as yourself.

God is _____

Love comes from _____

Since God loved us we should _____

Rebekah Farthing

God's love is made _____ in us.

We _____ and _____ on the love God has for us.

There is no _____ in love

We love because _____

Anyone who loves God must also _____.

Love is seen by the actions that are birthed from it.

LOVING GOD

Jesus answered him, "If a man loves me, he will keep my word.
My Father will love him, and we will come to him, and make our
home with him.

(John 14:23 WEB)

God has promised us if we obey His commandments He will come and live with us. How awesome
would it be to have God, the creator of the universe, living in your house?! To be able to sit and
have breakfast with Him every morning, to discuss His plans for that day, for that week, to come
home and have Him greet you or to be able to discuss whatever is weighing heavy on your heart.
Sounds nice doesn't it? I want to share something with you. ... You can have that.

For what great nation is there that has a god so near to them as
Yahweh our God is whenever we call on him?

(Deuteronomy 4:7 WEB)

By this we know that we remain in him and he in us, because he
has given us of his Spirit.

(1 John 4:13 WEB)

What agreement does a temple of God have with idols? For you are
a temple of the living God. Even as God said, "I will dwell in them
and walk in them. I will be their God and they will be my people.

(2 Corinthians 6:16 WEB)

He is with us. To think that He isn't would not be walking in truth. It would not be having
faith.

> Without faith it is impossible to be well pleasing to him, for he
> who comes to God must believe that he exists, and that he is a
> rewarder of those who seek him.
>
> (Hebrews 11:6 WEB)

We must believe God exists and that He abides with us.

You must believe in the spirit realm. That it is as real as this dimension. I can't see energy, but I know it exists. I see the evidence of it and can feel it when someone shocks me. The same is true with the spirit, you can't see it, but you can see the evidence of it and feel it. The spirit world is just as real as this world. Everything that happens in this dimension is a result of what happened in the spirit. Think about it, all our answers are answered first in another dimension and then we see the result of it. The fall of the angels was in the spirit dimension and it changed the course of our history. We are called to battle in the spirit dimension.

> For our wrestling is not against flesh and blood, but against the
> principalities, against the powers, against the world's rulers of the
> darkness of this age, and against the spiritual forces of wickedness
> in the heavenly places.
>
> (Ephesians 6:12 WEB)

God is ever present. I have a great Aunt and in her house at the living room table was a chair. Well, there were a few chairs, but this particular chair was special. It was Jesus' chair and no one else could sit in it. She would talk to Him and fellowship with Him because He was a living ever present savior to her — and that's what He should be to us. Does God need a chair? No, but He does want a place at your table. He does want fellowship with you. He wants to be acknowledged and present in your life; He wants an intimate relationship with you.

God is love. He speaks all the love languages and He desires to hear them too. There are 5 love languages; receiving gifts, quality time, words of affirmation, acts of service, and physical touch.

We have the opportunity to give these back to God.

Gifts:

We give to the church. We give of our possessions to the furthering of the kingdom. Be it food, finances, flowers … whatever you have.

Quality time:

God loves spending time with you! Go for a walk and talk with Him. Sit in His presence. Engage in praise. Push everything aside and say, "God, this is your time."

Words of affirmation:

This would be praise! Holy, Holy, Holy are you Lord almighty. Declare His greatness and goodness.

Acts of service:

What can you do for God? What skills has He given you that you can use for His glory?

Think outside the box.

What is the greatest command?

_____

What is the second one?

_____

If we love God, we will_____

We must believe God_____ and that He _____

_____

What are the 5 love languages?

_____

_____

What are some ways you can show God your love for Him?

_____

_____

_____

_____

What can change the world? _____

How can you show love to others? Come up with some ways that fit what you do and are realistic for you and the gifts and abilities you have.

_____
_____
_____
_____

LOVING OTHERS

The second is like this, 'You shall love your neighbor as yourself.
There is no other commandment greater than these.

(Mark 12:31 WEB)

What can change the world? Love. Since God is love, love in its forms is how we show Jesus to the world. We've looked at the love languages and how we can speak them to God to show Him our love, but let's look and see how we can show God's love to others.

Touch:

Be Jesus' hands. Lay hands on the sick. Give a hug to someone feeling down. Carry someone's groceries out to the car for them. Hold someone's hand who's going through a rough time. Sometimes people need a high five or a fist bump too!

Words:

Speak words of life into people. Only let that which is helpful to the building up of the body come out of your mouth. A lot of us don't share encouraging words because we're afraid of how we'll look or sound; that it will sound forced or even condescending. But a kind word is never ill-received. Give it a shot!

Gifts:

Is there something you make like jam or cards or lotion? Or even something you buy. Are you a great couponer or thrifter? Do you have any extra clothes in your closet that you really don't need, but you know someone who could use them? Sometimes we can share the love of Jesus with the simplest of gifts. Something that says, "you're not forgotten. You are thought of."

> Isn't it to distribute your bread to the hungry, and that you bring
> the poor who are cast out to your house? When you see the naked,
> that you cover him; and that you not hide yourself from your own
> flesh?
>
> (Isaiah 58:7 WEB)

All I can picture right now is the scene form *The Lord of The Rings* when Bilbo's relatives are knocking on the door, and he is hiding under the table trying to be quiet so they will go away. How often do we say we are "too busy" or we don't pick up the phone because that relative always wants something? Ouch! Hitting a little too close to home? God didn't call us to love the loveable, but the outcasts and the annoying people too.

Acts of service:

> "Don't withhold good from those to whom it is due, when it is in
> the power of your hand to do it."
>
> Proverbs 3:27 (WEB)

What needs do you see that you can meet? Does someone need help splitting wood? Does an elderly neighbor need help cleaning or cooking? Does that single mom you know need someone to watch her kids once or twice? Does someone need a ride to the grocery store or hospital? Find a need and fill it.

Quality time:

Go spend time with the least of these. Visit people who have been forgotten and let them know God didn't forget about them. Our time is not our own. The minute we gave our lives to Jesus, we gave Him every minute of it and we can't take it back now. If we want Him to be Lord of our lives, we are going to have to give Him the reins and let Him reign.

There was an instance where I was walking down my road talking to God and someone I knew pulled up and said, "hey, I know of this couple that doesn't have a car and they're new here and might need a ride a few times this week. Could you help?" I said sure at that moment, but as soon as they pulled away my flesh was thinking, "Oh man, now I've got to go chauffeur people around that I don't know on my days off. Great." Then it was like Jesus smacked me in the face. "You gave your life to me and said you'd do anything I wanted you to do. You are about to move 800 miles away because I told you to, but you're going to complain about doing this? You are not your own. You were bought with a price. My child, I'm going to need you to do all things without complaining." Yep, it stung a little. I felt horrible and repented right then and there. All ministry is important — not just the big glorious callings. You must be faithful with the little things. It's the dying to self and taking up your cross daily that defines the true follower of Christ.

My husband brought up a good point. If we show "love" with words or even actions out of obedience to the Lord but inwardly we are bitter is that really loving? Let's consider this verse on truth.

> My little children, let's not love in word only, or with the tongue
> only, but in deed and truth.
>
> (1 John 3:18 WEB)

This is truth in reality. So no, you cannot just go through the motions. If you have a grievance, grudge, bitterness within you, you need to take it to the Lord in prayer first before you can be a conduit with which the love of the Lord can flow. Sometimes you might not exactly feel like doing what the Spirit is telling you, but I believe these times are a test of obedience and a step of faith. The Lord will equip you with every good thing and every gift of the Spirit that you require to walk out what He has called you to do. Just like the parting of the Red Sea, it might start with a step from you before you see the provisions come.

All ministry is important not just the big glorious callings.

UNSELFISH LOVE

Once we show Jesus — that is, love — to people, it creates a door to tell them how Jesus performed the greatest act of love for them. That is what it's all about — introducing our savior and His kingdom to the world. Imagine you live in a mansion with Daddy Warbucks (from Annie) and there were many rooms and more than enough provisions to go around. Then Mr. Warbucks tells you to go find the kids who were like you that have no home and offer them a place to stay and an inheritance in the estate. Would you stay silent? Would you not go save your fellow orphans? That's a picture of our world, and our heavenly Father has many mansions and owns the cattle on a thousand hills. His resources never deplete. He's full of love, grace, and compassion. He is slow to anger and abounding in mercy. If we really have faith that He is who He says He is and that He does what He says He will, then why are we so ashamed of the gospel? Why do we keep it hidden under a bush? We must first seek the approval of God over the approval of man.

> For I am not ashamed of the Good News of Christ, because it is
> the power of God for salvation for everyone who believes, for the
> Jew first, and also for the Greek.
>
> (Romans 1:16 WEB)

The love that is going to save the world is the love that is Christ. On our own, we lack the capability to love people with the kind of love it takes to save the world — that's why we must be in love with Jesus first and abide in Him. In order to have that perfect love from the spirit. Perfect love casts out fear. When we are in His love, we can trust in it. We can know that He loves us and has our best in mind. If He tells us to go to a foreign country, or to a prison cell or to the streets of an inner city, He's got us, and we don't have to be afraid. If we want the love He has for the lost and hurting, we should ask for it. I know I'm not perfect and I am far from where I should be so agape loving people is not my first nature. I constantly pray to be filled more and more with His spirit so I would abound in the gifts of the spirit (mainly love and kindness) and that God would give me a love for those that are hard to love. It's easy to look at the face of a child who has been living under the oppression of a warlord and love on them, but how easy is it to look into the grimaced hardened face of the warlord and show love?

I was recently brought to tears as I read a story of a ten year old girl who was in a slave camp in India. She worked all day for one meal and was sexually abused every night by her captor. The people that got her out of that horrid situation said they prayed for the captor and even tried to share the gospel with him. I don't want you to miss that. They prayed for and tried to share the gospel with the man that was torturing this child. My heart was filled with anger at this man and I began to think of all the slow painful ways death could be inflicted as seemingly just punishment. You can't honestly say you haven't thought the same thing at one point. Then the still small voice said, "love him." Excuse me? Say *WHAT*? Really? No! And yet again He spoke, "love them".

I then began to cry as I fought with my soul to release the anger and bitterness I had towards this man and all others like him.

We, as humans, are ALL God's creation, made in His image. He desires ALL to come to repentance and know Him as father. Often, we justify our hatred for individuals as righteous anger. I mean they're of the devil, right? That's our enemy and they're working for him!

Reel yourself in. That person, who we are hating for his acts, is a creation of God. When he was born, he was born into sin like the rest of us, but instead of seeing and coming to know Christ, the devil kidnapped him, made him a prisoner of war, and brainwashed him by creating circumstances that would blind him to the Father's love, desire for relationship, and the purpose on his life. He isn't of the devil. He's been overcome by the forces of darkness. Remember everything we see in this world is a result of something happening in the spirit world. The spirit of lust has tormented many and caused them to do horrible things. These people still have the choice to follow through or fight these feelings and suggestions by evil spirits, but without the Holy Spirit as your guide and conscience, many get overcome.

If you've ever watched or read *The Hunger Games*, I want you to recall Peeta. He was the sweetest person, who loved Katniss despite her flighty indecisive behavior. The enemy used this love against him. He captured Peeta brainwashed him and released him. Peeta became an angry, enraged, person out to destroy Katniss and the rebels he once fought beside. The rebels ended up rescuing him and tying him down in a hospital. Every day they would try to reverse the effects of the brainwashing and tell him the truth. It took a long time for him to be retrained — to re-learn who he was — but Katniss refused to give up on him because she had developed a true love for him. This is a picture of a love that sees past the effects of the enemy devices and to the person that is deep inside there.

God wants us to love everybody.

This is the love God wants us to have for other people. A love that will say, "I won't give up on you, because God has not given up on you."

> Beloved, let's love one another, for love is of God; and everyone
> who loves has been born of God, and knows God.
>
> (1 John 4:7 WEB)

If we do not love, we merely know about God. We do not truly know or have a personal relationship with God. I know about Joyce Meyers, I know her voice, what she looks like and her background, but do I know her personally? No! It's like that with God. We can know what he says, memorize verses, recognize when He does something incredible, but if we don't love we aren't in a relationship with Him. When we are in a relationship, we will be so filled with love that it will pour out of us.

> By this everyone will know that you are my disciples, if you have
> love for one another.
>
> (John 13:35 WEB)

This love is the agape love. What does agape love look like walked out? We are given a list of the characteristics of this love in 1 Corinthians.

> Love is patient and is kind. Love doesn't envy. Love doesn't brag,
> is not proud, doesn't behave itself inappropriately, doesn't seek its
> own way, is not provoked, takes no account of evil; doesn't rejoice
> in unrighteousness, but rejoices with the truth; bears all things,
> believes all things, hopes all things, and endures all things.
>
> (1 Corinthians 13:4-7 WEB)

This is how we should be described. Disciples of Jesus are patient (long suffering), they are kind, they don't covet other people's stuff or lives, they're not jealous, they do not go around flaunting their things, social status, or money. Followers of Jesus do not behave rudely, especially to your waiter or waitress. (It's actually known among the public service realm that Sundays are the worst days to work because the church people are some of the most impatient rude, puffed up people there are. WE NEED TO CHANGE THIS!)

They put the welfare of others first, aren't easily offended, don't wish evil on others (You mean they have control of their thoughts? Yup.) Jesus' disciples do not get excited when people are walking out the consequences of their actions.

Imagine if you will, you have 2 kids. 1 of them lies to you. Thus, he must walk out his consequence. The other kid starts laughing and saying, "nah nah, you got in trouble." Now you kindly want to tell the other kid next time he is in trouble you will not show him any mercy because he did not look upon his sibling with mercy. He is rejoicing in the others iniquity. Oh, how that breaks our Father's heart. He doesn't like punishing His children but there are consequences to actions.

Finally, His disciples bear all things, believe all things, hope all things, endure all things. You are able to bear any trial because the Spirit is within you and equips you. You believe all things the Lord speaks. You hope in Him, and you endure whatever comes your way.

We want to be lights. We want to show Jesus to those around us. We should anyways, it's what we're called to do. It's our love that will set us apart. Not how many services we attend throughout the week, not how many verses we memorize, but our love. Begin to cultivate love for those around you by asking God to help you see people the way He sees them. Trust me it doesn't come naturally or easy. And it can get used up, so be sure to renew your love tank every day by going to the Father in prayer and in worship.

God want us to love _____

How do we prove to the world that we are His disciples?

_____

1 John 4:7 (WEB)- " Beloved, let's _____ one another, for _____ is of _____;
and everyone who _____ has been _____ of God, and _____ God."

What will save the world? _____

Perfect love _____

Love is:

Love is P_ _ _ _ _ _ _

is K _ _ _

love does not _ _ _ _

love does not _ _ _ _

it is not _ _ _ _ _

does not behave _ _ _ _ _ _ _ _ _ _ _ _ _ _ _,

is not p _ o _ o _ ed,

no account of _ _ _ _

Rejoices with the _ _ _ _ _

H _ _ _ _ all things, and endures all things.

Are you justifying hatred as righteous anger?

Is there anything you need to confess to Jesus and repent of?

Now's the time.

WE MUST FIRST SEEK THE APPROVAL OF GOD OVER THE APPROVAL OF MAN.

THE END OF THE BEGINNING

I hope through all of this you have gained a greater understanding
of who God is and who He wants you to be.

This world needs super heroes. Will you answer the call?

Will you choose to lay aside the comfy life and become warriors? Will you fight for Justice? Will you extend Mercy? Will you act in ways that make people wonder? Will you be a woman of God that is peculiar to the kingdom of Heaven? So that when people see you they see and recognize the dress you wear, and the fragrance of Christ. The battle is at our doorstep. We can't afford to be lukewarm — to hide in the foxhole and wait till the battle's over. God tells us we have the victory already. He tells us this not to give us an excuse to stay out of the battle, but to give us hope and strength through it.

Rise up Women of Wonder and take the place of Wonder Women you were created for! I have made a declaration based on all that we have learned. I hope you will make one for yourself too and place it somewhere you can see it.

I am Princess Rebekah of the kingdom of heaven. Daughter of Adonai.

I will strive to show love to all those around me

I will walk daily with my Father in heaven

I will fight the good fight for the kingdom of heaven

I will take up my sword of the spirit which is the word of God

and wield it against the powers of darkness

I will hold up my shield of faith and run behind it

No weapon formed against me shall prosper because I am the Lord's

By God's grace I will be all that he needs me to be

I am a woman of wonder

Printed in the United States
by Baker & Taylor Publisher Services